The Distribution of Income in California

. . .

Deborah Reed

Melissa Glenn Haber

Laura Mameesh

JULY 1996

PUBLIC POLICY INSTITUTE OF CALIFORNIA

ISBN: 0-9653184-0-0

Foreword

This report on income distribution is the first research publication of the Public Policy Institute of California (PPIC). In developing the initial research agenda for the institute, we focused on fundamental changes that are sweeping the state. Of the many possibilities, one area that clearly deserved a place on our list is the dramatically changing nature of the state's economy.

California has emerged from its deepest recession since the 1930s. The economy is expanding steadily, with hundreds of thousands of jobs being created annually. In the bloom of this recovery, it makes sense to step back and look at the changes in the distribution of income in California that have occurred in recent years and over the last several decades.

Recent efforts to measure and explain changes in income distribution in the United States have generated considerable interest and debate. This report is the first in a series that will replicate for California much of the national-level analysis. The authors document, for the first time, the annual changes in income distribution in the state from the late 1960s through 1994. Subsequent reports will examine the causes of increasing inequality, exploring the role of such factors as technological change, international competition, immigration, deunionization, and the shifting demographics of California.

We trust that these reports not only will improve our understanding of the economic changes under way in California but will signal PPIC's commitment to high-quality research and analyses useful to policy audiences.

The authors express their appreciation to Sheldon Danziger from the University of Michigan and Lynn Karoly from RAND for their timely and extensive comments on an earlier draft. Lori Dair and John Ellwood were essential to the production of this report. Patricia Bedrosian, Jerry Lubenow, and Joyce Peterson provided considerable editorial assistance. The study has benefited from the efforts of Janet DeLand, Rod Pedersen, Eileen Roush, Peg Schumacher, Michael Shires, Karen Steeber, Michael Teitz, Paul Tractenberg, and numerous colleagues at PPIC. While this report reflects the contributions of many people, the authors are solely responsible for its content.

David W. Lyon
President and CEO
Public Policy Institute of California

Summary

In recent years, increasing inequality in the distribution of income has been a subject of considerable public concern, political attention, and academic research. Income inequality is a measure of how equally the income pie is divided among all members of society. In other words, it is a measure of *relative* income, gauging, for example, how well the poor are doing economically compared with the rich.

In the United States, income inequality remained stable in the three decades that followed World War II, as rich and poor alike benefited from the nation's growing affluence. By the 1960s, Americans had come to accept as an article of faith President John Kennedy's assertion that a rising tide would lift all boats. However, since the early 1970s the gap separating the rich and the poor has grown wider.

While national studies have documented a growth in income inequality throughout the 1970s and 1980s, relatively little research has been done on income distribution in California. Such research is crucial to the reasoned resolution of a broad range of state issues such as tax policy, public education, the minimum wage, and welfare reform that both affect and are affected by the distribution of income.

The well-being of California's population is a major research theme of the Public Policy Institute of California. This report is the first in a series that aims to identify state-specific policy strategies to promote equity as well as growth in the state's economy. This initial study documents trends in income distribution in California from 1967 to 1994 and compares them to trends in other states, other regions, and the nation as a whole. Successive studies will investigate the underlying causes of the trends and will examine the relationship between public policy and the distribution of income.

In this summary, we discuss the major findings of the study that, we believe, will be of interest to general and policy audiences concerned with important state issues. The body of the report and the appendices describe in greater detail the study's results, approaches, measures, and data sources. We have striven to make the discussion in all parts of the report accessible to all interested audiences.

Summing Up the Picture of California Income Inequality

Income inequality has increased steadily in California over the last three decades. Until the late 1980s, the trend in California was remarkably similar to the national trend but, since then, inequality has risen much faster in the state than in the nation. This change has held for adjusted household incomes and for male earnings but not for female earnings.

In both California and the nation, the increasing inequality results from income growth at the top of the distribution and decline in incomes at the very bottom. However, the recent divergence in inequality trends between California and the nation does not arise from faster growth at the top in California: In fact, income growth at all levels has been slower in California. Instead, the greater increase in the state results from a precipitous drop in income at the mid-to-lowest levels of the distribution.

Rapid growth in income inequality has coincided with business cycle recessions, with those at the lower levels especially hard hit during recessions. A crucial difference has been that in the nation at large, incomes of people at those levels rebounded more during business cycle upswings than they did in California. However, the inequality gap between the nation and California began to widen as early as 1987, even before the recent, deep recession.

These results suggest that in the interest of equity and economic growth in the state, it is essential that future research identify the forces that have made people at the lower end of the distribution lose so much ground and examine what happened in California even before the most recent recession.

More on the Study's Major Findings

In this study, we used five summary measures of inequality, 26 definitions of income, and two data series (the Current Population Survey and the Census) to analyze California income levels and trends and to compare them with national and regional levels and trends. Our major findings are summarized below.

Income Inequality Has Increased Substantially in California

Figure S.1 illustrates how much the distribution of annual earnings has widened among male workers in California. The middle line of the graph shows the percentage change in real, inflation-adjusted median male earnings since 1967. The lower line of the figure shows the decline of male earnings at the 20th percentile, the income level that separates the bottom 20 percent of earners from the top 80 percent. The upper line of the figure shows the growing earnings at the 80th percentile.

As shown in Figure S.1, the median of male earnings fell 20 percent between 1967 and 1994. This 20 percent decline represents a drop in median male earnings from $31,252 to $25,000 in real 1994 dollars. At

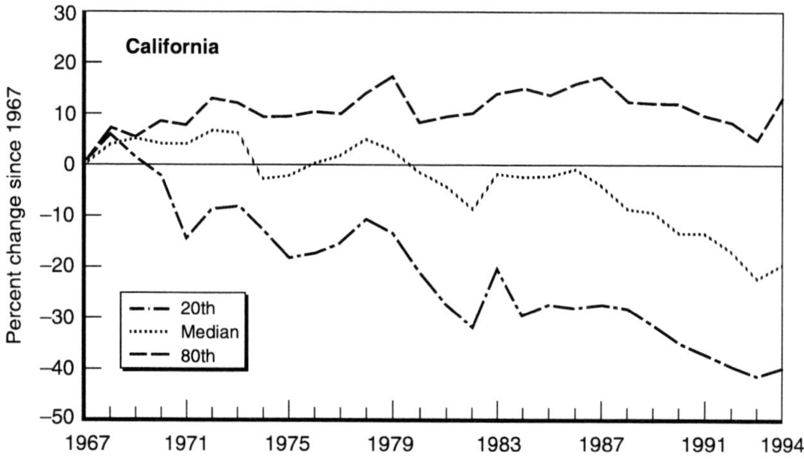

SOURCE: Based on authors' calculations from the March CPS.

NOTE: Sample includes civilians age 18 and older who received wage and salary income. Statistics reported in this figure are adjusted for inflation.

Figure S.1—Percentage Change in Real Annual Earnings for Males in California, by Income Percentile, 1967–1994

the 20th percentile, male earnings fell 40 percent from $17,316 in 1967 to $10,400 in 1994. In 1967, a man at the 80th percentile earned $44,345, about two and a half times what a man at the 20th percentile earned. By 1994, male earnings at the 80th percentile had increased 13 percent to $50,000, about five times what a man at the 20th percentile earned in that year. This comparison of the earnings of men in the upper-middle to the lower-middle of the distribution—the 80/20 ratio—is one simple measure of inequality. By this measure, male earnings inequality increased by 88 percent between 1967 and 1994 in California.

Although the 80/20 ratio is an intuitive measure of inequality, it captures only two points in the distribution of income. Other measures of inequality are preferable because they summarize the entire distribution of income including the extreme top and bottom. One such measure is the coefficient of variation (CV). By this measure, male earnings inequality increased 41 percent between 1967 and 1994. Even by 1989, before the most recent recession, inequality had increased 35 percent since 1967.

Income Inequality in California Matched That of the Nation Until the Late 1980s

Inequality in household income has also grown. As Figure S.2 shows, household income inequality was similar in California and the nation for most of the years studied: It fluctuated in the 1970s, increasing during recessions and declining in recovery. It shot up dramatically during the recession of the early 1980s and never returned to pre-recession levels. It then remained fairly stable at new, higher levels through the mid-1980s.

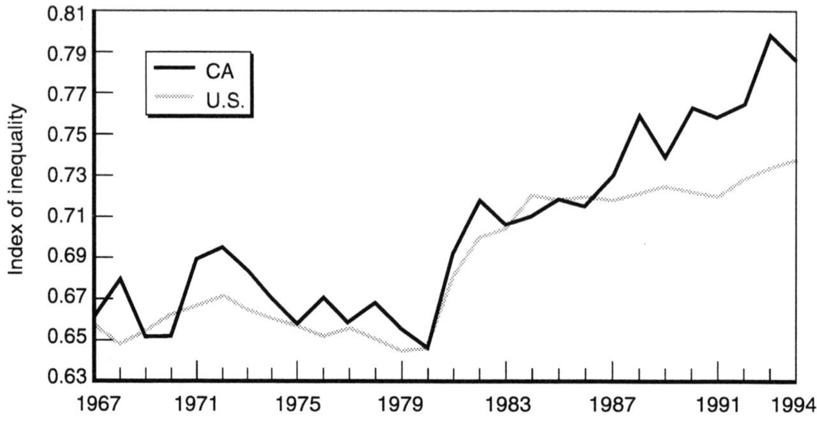

SOURCE: Authors' calculations from the March CPS.

NOTE: Household income is adjusted for household size and weighted by person. Statistics in this figure are not affected by inflation. The index of inequality used is the coefficient of variation (CV). The CV is the standard deviation of income divided by the mean of income.

Figure S.2—Household Income Inequality in California and the Nation, 1967–1994

The trend in California's income inequality began to diverge from the national trend in 1987. Inequality in household income started to increase faster in the state than in the nation, with especially rapid increases during the most recent recession. The period beginning in the late 1980s stands out as the only time when California has had substantially higher household income inequality than the nation for so many consecutive years. This divergence is also found in male earnings but not in female earnings.

The fast-rising trend of inequality in California is also markedly visible when compared with other states. In 1969, 20 states had higher household income and male earnings inequality. By 1989, only five states had higher household income inequality and only two had higher male earnings inequality.

Income in California Has Grown More Slowly at the Top and Declined More Rapidly at the Bottom

The sharp divergence between the state and the nation is not the result of higher income growth for the rich in California. As Figure S.3 shows, household income grew more in the nation than in the state. Between 1969 and 1989, two peak years of the business cycle, household income at the 90th percentile grew by 42 percent in the nation and 31 percent in the state. Instead, the divergence results from a greater income decline at the bottom. At the 10th percentile, while income in the nation grew by 7 percent, it actually fell by 7 percent in California.

Incorporating data from the most recent recession shows an even more dramatic difference in growth between the nation and the state, as seen in the lower panel of the figure. Between the business cycle troughs of 1976 and 1994, income levels at the median and below fell in California, but in the United States they fell only at the 10th and 20th percentiles. Moreover, the decline in income at the 10th percentile in the United States was not nearly so drastic as in the state: Nationally, income fell by 8 percent, but in California, it fell by a remarkable 30 percent.

Rapid Growth in Income Inequality Coincided with Business Cycle Recessions

In both California and the nation, rapid growth in inequality coincided with recessions. The most noticeable increases in household income inequality, for example, occurred during the recessions of the early 1970s, early 1980s, and early 1990s. To illustrate, inequality in

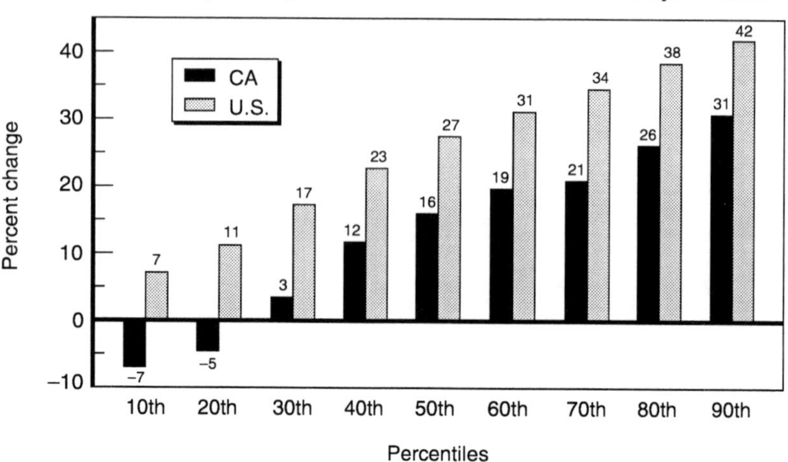

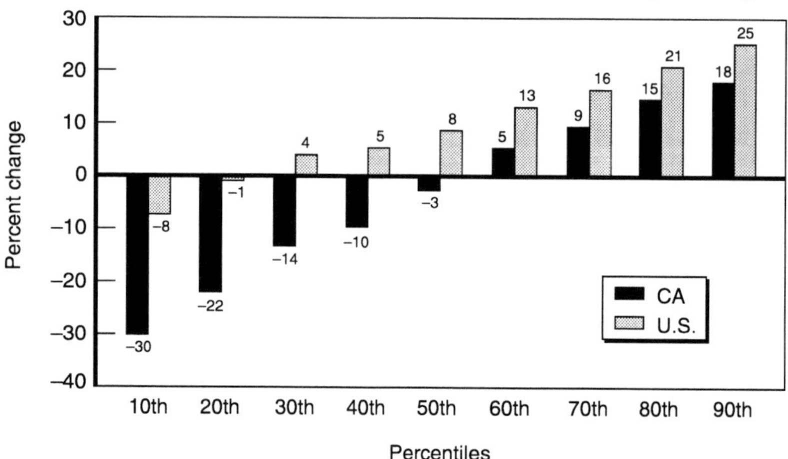

SOURCE: Based on authors' calculations from the March CPS.

NOTES: Household income is adjusted for household size and weighted by persons. Statistics in this figure are adjusted for inflation.

Figure S.3—Percentage Change in Household Income Between Selected Years

adjusted household income increased by 9 percent in California during the 1979–1982 recession, but it increased by only 3 percent during the economic growth of the next seven years. The relationship between the business cycle and inequality is particularly strong for male annual earnings in California: Inequality increased by 13 percent between 1979 and 1982 but by only 1 percent between 1982 and 1989.

The recessions of the early 1970s and 1990s hit California harder than the nation (as is reflected in the larger increases in inequality shown in Figure S.2). While much of the rapid rise in inequality since 1981 occurred during the recession of the early 1990s, not all of the difference between California and the nation can be attributed to the strength of the recession in the state. The California growth trend in inequality began to outpace the national trend even before the start of the recession.

Considering the Implications

While inequality can increase because of the unequal sharing of income growth, it is particularly disturbing when it arises because of a decline in the income of poor individuals and households. This is the pattern that has characterized the increasing inequality in California over the last three decades.

It is important to note, however, that the results of the study do not indicate that people who were poor in the past have gotten poorer—nor, conversely, that none have prospered. People who were in the 20th percentile in 1967 could have been in the 80th percentile in 1994. The data for this analysis are cross-sectional (snapshots of those in income groups in each year), not longitudinal, and therefore do not follow the fortunes of specific families or individuals over time. What the analysis does tell us is that the poor in 1994 were considerably worse off than the poor in 1967. Moreover, as income falls at the bottom of the distribution, a greater percentage of people fall below the official poverty line (or any other absolute level of need). In other words, more Californians are poor today than were poor in the late 1960s.

Given the similar trends in income inequality in California and the nation, it seems likely that the same forces are at work in both. Research on the underlying causes at the national level suggests a combination of factors: labor market trends influenced by technological change, international competition, immigration, and deunionization; and demographic trends in marriage and female employment. If these same forces explain the rise in inequality in the state, however, the recent sharp divergence suggests possible differential effects of those forces in California.

Some Americans believe that differences in income arise primarily from individual choices, preferences, abilities, investments, and productivity, and that income inequality is a product of an economy that values hard work and talent. Other Americans believe that income differences reflect the unequal distribution of economic opportunity in our society, and that the opportunity to succeed is elusive for those who do not belong to privileged groups. The first viewpoint implies that public policy can affect inequality only by redistributing income; the second implies that policy can reduce inequality by promoting opportunity. Research on the determinants of the income distribution and the extent to which policy provides or restricts economic opportunity will suggest avenues for improving opportunities for the less-advantaged.

Continuing growth in inequality is not inevitable. It is evident that government policies do affect the distribution of income, although the mechanisms are not fully understood. The challenge for future research is to examine the underlying forces behind the recent growth in inequality and to identify state policies that can promote equity and opportunity, as well as efficiency, in the California economy.

Contents

Figures

Tables

1. Introduction

A fuller understanding of state-level trends in the distribution of income is essential for California. The recent trends not only will determine the need for strengthened state policies to aid low-income families but will affect the likely success of those policies.

This report provides a comprehensive description of the widening distribution of income in California. Its findings reveal a general pattern of increasing income inequality in the state, explained by a dramatic decline in income for the poor and near-poor accompanied by income growth for the rich. Subsequent studies by the Public Policy Institute of California will examine the underlying causes of the trends and will explore the relationships between state policy and income inequality.

Trends in Income Inequality

The upward trend in income inequality in the United States throughout the 1970s and 1980s stands in marked contrast with the trends in the distribution of income from the Great Depression to the late 1960s. Jeffrey Williamson and Peter Lindert (1980) report a dramatic decline in income inequality between the Depression and the end of World War II. From the late 1940s until the late 1970s, inequality fluctuated within a relatively narrow band. This long period of stability in income inequality led to speculation that, with the exception of short-term fluctuations, the distribution of economic well-being would remain constant (Blinder, 1980). Tracking changes in inequality, wrote one researcher, was like "watching grass grow" (Aaron, 1978, p. 17).

The conventional wisdom was too optimistic. In the early 1980s, Census Bureau reports provided some of the earliest indications of a growing inequality among families. Census Bureau income statistics revealed that family income inequality had reached a postwar low in the late 1960s but had climbed almost constantly from that time. Since the early 1980s, family income inequality has remained higher than in any previous year since the end of the Second World War.[1]

In recent years, numerous studies have documented the widening distribution of family income and male earnings in the United States. We summarize this work here. Sheldon Danziger and Peter Gottschalk (1995) report that the gap in income between families near the top of the income distribution and those near the bottom has increased, in both recession and recovery, since the recession of the early 1970s. The years 1983 to 1989 stand out as an anomalous period that recorded growth in mean family income along with rising income inequality.

---

[1] U.S. Bureau of the Census, *Current Population Reports*, P-60 series, various issues.

In their comprehensive 1992 review article, Frank Levy and
Richard Murnane conclude that the 1970s were a period of either
stability or gradual growth in male annual earnings inequality and that
the 1980s were a period of rapid increase. Lynn Karoly (1993) shows
that this rise in income inequality is explained by a decline in the
income of poor families and workers and by growth in the income of the
rich.

While much attention has been focused on the trends in income
inequality at the national level, relatively few studies have investigated
income distribution in the state of California. There are many reasons to
expect that the trends in the distribution of income in California will
differ from those of the nation. Income inequality measures for the
country as a whole aggregate regional diversity in economic and
demographic trends. California is distinctive in its industrial base,
trading partners, racial and ethnic composition, patterns of domestic
and international migration, and in the age and education of its
workforce.

Previous research on the distribution of income in California shows
that the state has experienced a rise in income disparity. Jay Chamberlain
and Phil Spillberg (1991) report a rising concentration of adjusted gross
income in the 1980s: Between 1980 and 1988, the proportion of the
total after-tax adjusted income received by the top 20 percent of taxpayers
increased from 52 to 57 percent; the proportion received by the top *one*
percent increased from 10 to 16 percent. Karoly (1995) finds that the
ratio of the income of wealthy families at the 90th percentile to the
income of poor families at the 10th percentile—the 90/10 ratio—

increased by 74 percent between 1973 and 1993 in California.[2] This rise in inequality was due to growth in the incomes of the rich and a substantial decline in the incomes of the poor. Moreover, the rise in inequality in California was larger than in the nation as a whole, where the 90/10 ratio increased by 54 percent.

Research that compares California to other regions of the country is less conclusive. On the one hand, Robert Topel (1994) finds that the western region of the nation, dominated in population by California, experienced the largest increase of any region in male wage inequality between 1972 and 1990. On the other hand, Thomas Husted (1991) shows that between 1981 and 1987, the percentage increase in the Gini coefficient (one index of inequality) was higher in California than in the nation as a whole, but 24 states had larger percentage increases.

Nature of the Study

This study contributes to the existing research on the distribution of income in California by providing a comprehensive description of state trends and by comparing these to trends of the nation, other regions, and other states. To document the trends in income inequality thoroughly, the study uses five measures of inequality and 26 definitions of income. Data for this analysis come from the annual March file of the Current Population Survey and the decennial Census of Population and

---

[2]The 10th percentile is defined as the level of income that divides the bottom 10 percent from the top 90 percent; similarly, 90 percent of people have incomes below the 90th percentile, whereas only 10 percent have incomes above.

Housing.[3] The analysis covers the entire period spanned by available public-use files of the Current Population Survey: 1967 to 1994.

This study measures the trends for two main types of income: *Household income* provides a picture of general economic well-being because it includes all sources of money income and it is measured for all people regardless of work status. *Labor income*, the largest component of household income, measures earnings from work. Labor income reflects changes in the economy and is not directly influenced by changes in household structure.

The next two chapters describe results of the study. Chapter 2 describes trends in the distribution of household income and Chapter 3 describes trends in the distribution of male and female labor income. Each chapter analyzes the California experience in relation to that of other regions and states. Chapter 4 presents our conclusions, discusses the relationship between public policy and the distribution of income, and outlines possible explanations for the rise of income inequality in California.

Readers interested in greater technical details of the study are directed to the appendices: Appendix A describes the datasets used in the study. Appendix B discusses the representativeness of the California subsample of the Current Population Survey. Appendix C reports on trends in the distribution of alternative measures of income. Appendix D provides supplementary statistics on the distributions of income measures discussed in the text.

------

[3]1970 Public Use Sample, 1 percent, and the 1980 and 1990 Public Use Micro Sample, 5 percent.

2. Trends in the Distribution of Household Income

Household income is a measure of economic well-being that explicitly accounts for income-sharing among members of the same household. It is the most comprehensive measure of income in this study because it is measured for all people regardless of age and work status, and it incorporates income from all reported sources. As this chapter demonstrates, the distribution of household income in California has widened considerably over the past three decades, especially during business cycle recessions. Summary measures of inequality show that the increasing trend in household income inequality was similar for California and the nation until the late 1980s. Since then, the rise in inequality has been much greater in California. Compared to other states, California had one of the highest levels of inequality, even before the recent recession.

What Is Household Income?

Household income is defined as the sum of income from all sources for all persons living in the same household unit. Because households with many persons require more resources than small households to maintain the same level of consumption, we adjust household income based on the number of household residents.[1] We evaluate the distribution of adjusted household income across people, rather than across household units, by assigning to each person the adjusted income of his or her household. This method treats each person equally, rather than implicitly giving less weight in the calculation to people in large households.[2]

All income statistics reported in this study are adjusted to real 1994 dollars based on the consumer price index computed by the Bureau of Labor Statistics.[3] Recent studies suggest that the official consumer price index may exaggerate inflation, thus understating growth and overstating

---

[1] We calculate adjusted household income by dividing total household income by the square root of the number of household residents. Karoly and Burtless (1995) suggest this adjustment factor because it is close to the adjustment for family size implicit in the official poverty thresholds. This adjustment takes into account "economies of scale" made possible through the sharing of common resources in large households. For example, the adjustment implies that a household with four people will require twice, rather than four times, the income of a single person to maintain the same level of consumption. We make the same adjustments to family income based on family size. Median levels of adjusted household and family income reported in the text are multiplied by two to represent income levels for households and families of four persons. For comparison, we also measure changes in the distribution of unadjusted household and family income (see Appendix C).

[2] Using this method, 50 percent of people live in households with adjusted incomes lower than the median, as opposed to 50 percent of households falling below the median. Similarly, we evaluate the distribution of adjusted family income across people as opposed to family units. For comparison, we measure trends in the distributions of household income across households and family income across families (see Appendix C).

[3] We use the CPI U X1 and allow for differences in the rate of inflation in California and the United States. See Appendix A for details.

decline. However, although the consumer price index affects estimated growth trends, the summary measures of inequality used in this report are based on relative income (e.g., the income of the rich relative to the income of the poor) and are not affected by inflation adjustments.

The Current Population Survey and the Census report pre-tax money income including wages and salary, farm income, self-employment income, interest and dividends, welfare receipts, and Social Security and retirement benefits. The income measures are imperfect indices of economic well-being because the data do not include information on tax payments, non-monetary transfers (e.g., housing subsidies, health benefits, food stamps), the return to investments such as owner-occupied housing, or measures of accumulated wealth. However, studies that have used more comprehensive measures of income have found trends in income inequality similar to those for pre-tax money income. (See Appendix C for a review of such studies.)

Adjusted Household Income Is Sensitive to the Business Cycle

Because the business cycle plays a strong role in the distributional trends we describe, we begin by showing business cycle fluctuations as measured by unemployment and associated fluctuations in household income. Figure 2.1 shows how strongly fluctuations in adjusted household income are related to the business cycle. The upper panel of the figure displays the unemployment rate in California and the United States from 1967 to 1994. Rising rates of unemployment characterize the periods of recession of the early 1970s, mid-1970s, early 1980s, and

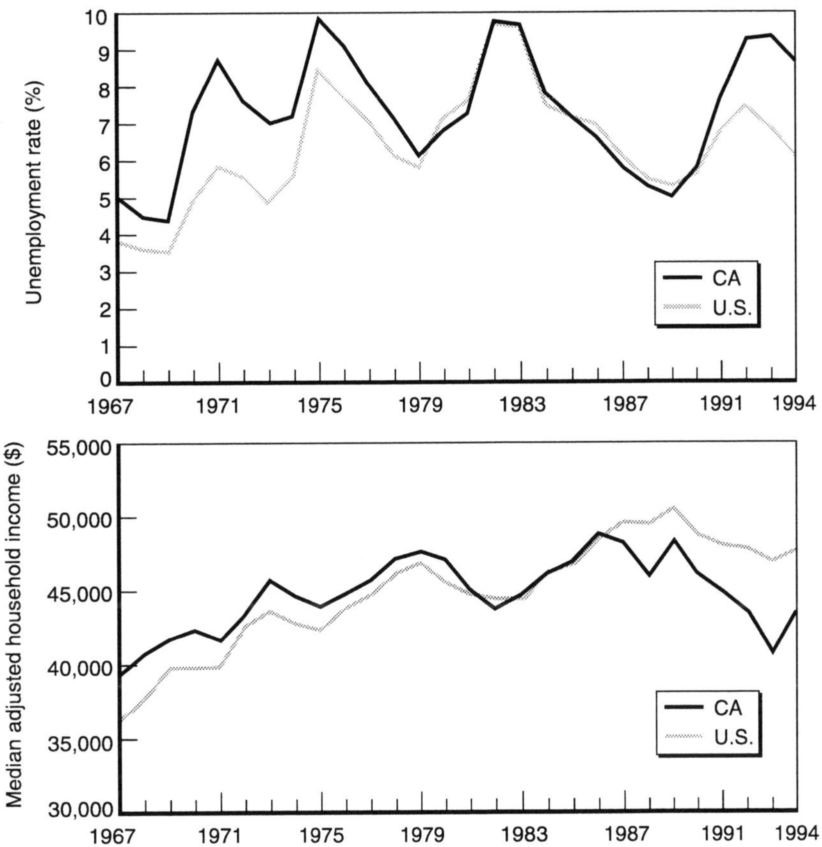

SOURCE: Real median adjusted household income is based on authors' calculations from the March CPS. Unemployment rates are from the Bureau of Labor Statistics.

NOTES: Median incomes have been converted to real 1994 dollars. The U.S. median has been adjusted to reflect the higher cost of living in California. Comparison of median income in California to median income in the United States should be made with caution because of measurement problems in the cost of living index (as described in Appendix A). The trend in median household income is sensitive to the consumer price index. Household income is adjusted for the number of people living in the household. Reported median household income is calibrated to represent a household of four people. Median household income in California in 1988 may not be comparable to other years due to changes in the CPS (as described in Appendix A).

Figure 2.1—Trends in the Unemployment Rate and Median Real Adjusted Household Income, 1967–1994

early 1990s for both California and the nation. With the exception of the 1980s, unemployment has been higher in California than in the nation, particularly during the recessions of the early 1970s and early 1990s.

Median adjusted household income (the lower panel of Figure 2.1) shows a positive growth trend through the mid-1980s for both California and the nation, with higher overall growth in the nation.[4] Declines in median household income generally occurred only during periods of recession. However, median household income in California began to stagnate as early as 1987, even before the most recent recession. The greater decline in median household income and the higher unemployment rate in California indicate the stronger effect of the early 1990s recession in the state. (The dip in median household income in 1988 is probably explained by changes in sampling in the Current Population Survey. Results for 1988 are reported in this study but conclusions are not based on statistics specific to 1988.)[5]

The medians in Figure 2.1 are adjusted both for inflation and for the higher cost of living in California. The position of the Californian median relative to the national median is a function of the adjustments

---

[4]If no adjustments were made to household income for household size and if the distribution were evaluated at the household level and not the person level, the median in the United States would be less than 1 percent higher than the median in California in 1994. The median of unadjusted household income (weighted at the household level) increased in the United States relative to California from 1967 to 1978; after 1978, the relative growth of the U.S. median fluctuated with no clear trend. However, the median of adjusted household income (weighted by persons), the median reported in the text, is a preferred measure of economic well-being because it accounts for the greater resource needs of large households and it applies the same weight to people in large households as to people in small households.

[5]See Appendix A for further discussion of sampling and other data issues.

made for differences in the cost of living.[6] For example, in 1994 the cost of living estimate was 9 percent higher in California than in the nation. The cost of living adjustments applied in this figure are calculated from Bureau of Labor Statistics data.[7] Because cost of living estimates are imprecise, comparison of the California median to the national median should be made with caution.

Although Figure 2.1 shows that the U.S. median adjusted household income was about $3,000 below that of California in 1967 and was about $4,000 above that of California in 1994, this result could be different if a more accurate cost of living index were available. However, the faster rise in the U.S. median does not depend on the cost of living adjustment. The median adjusted household income statistics in Figure 2.1 are the only statistics in this report that are affected by the cost of living adjustment.

The Distribution of Household Income Has Widened, Especially During Recessions

The most significant widening of the distribution of adjusted household income occurred during periods of recession, particularly in the early 1980s and early 1990s. Overall, the gap between the incomes of people in rich and poor households increased not only because incomes at the top of the distribution rose but also because incomes at the bottom of the distribution fell.

---

[6]For example, if no adjustments were made for cost of living, the median of adjusted household income in the United States would be about half a percent lower than the median in California in 1994. See Appendix D for the nominal value of income at each decile without adjustments for cost of living.

[7]See Appendix A for the calculation of cost of living adjustment for 1967–1994.

A straightforward way to investigate the changing shape of the distribution of income is to examine the relative income positions of low-, middle-, and high-income people. Figure 2.2 illustrates the income trends at the 10th, 20th, 50th (median), 80th, and 90th percentiles of adjusted household income.[8] The figure shows the percentage change in income since 1967: For example, the highest point on the graph for California shows that people in the 90th percentile in 1987 had income slightly more than 40 percent higher than people in the 90th percentile in 1967.

Although the reported statistics are standardized to the base year of 1967, the figure is not meant to imply that there was no household income inequality in 1967.[9] Instead, the figure graphically represents the widening of the distribution and corresponding increases in inequality from its 1967 levels.

The absolute decline of income levels for households near the bottom of the distribution in California is a striking feature of the figure. During the 1970s, the income received by households at the 10th and 20th percentiles of the distribution in California fluctuated mildly but showed little overall growth. During the recession of the early 1980s, the

---

[8]People in the 10th percentile have incomes higher than only 10 percent of the population; those in the 90th percentile have incomes higher than 90 percent of the population. People in the 10th and 20th percentiles are in the lower and lower-middle ranks of the income distribution; the median (or 50th percentile) describes the income level of people in the middle of the income distribution; the 80th and 90th percentiles indicate the income levels of people in the upper-middle and upper ranks of the income distribution.

[9]The information in the figure can be used to calculate the percentage change between any two years by using the following calculation: Add 100 to the values displayed on the figure, take the ratio, subtract 1, and multiply by 100. For example, between the business cycle peaks in 1979 and 1989, adjusted household income at the 10th percentile fell by 8 percent in California $(100/108.5 - 1) * 100$.

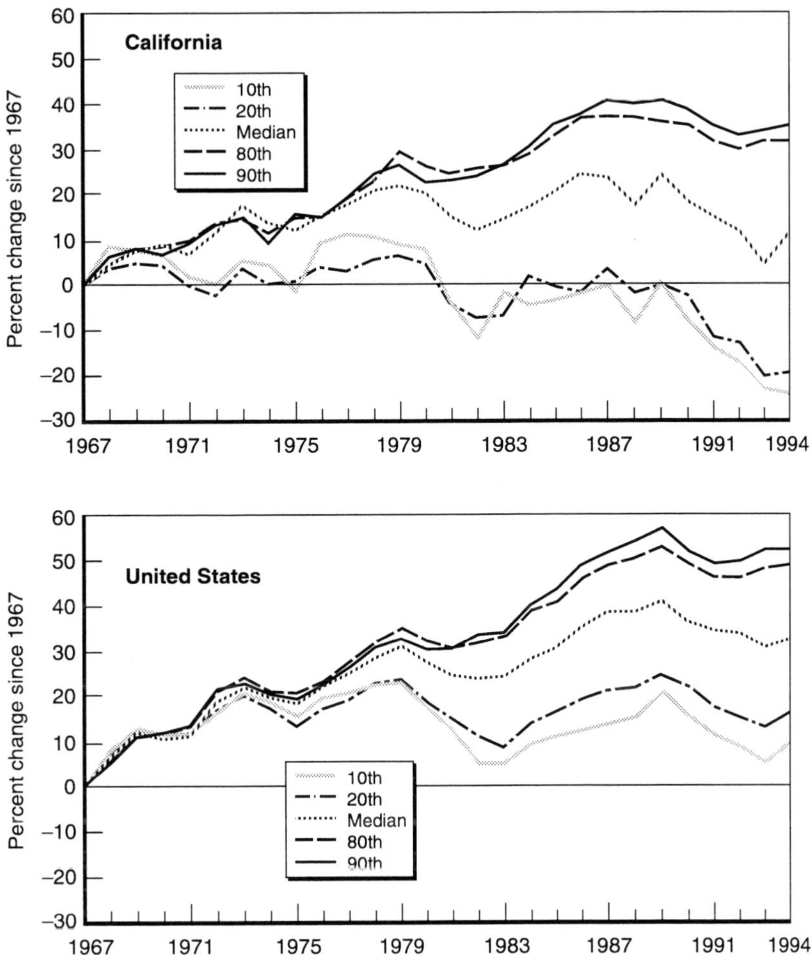

SOURCE: Based on authors' calculations from the March CPS.

NOTES: Statistics reported in this figure are sensitive to the consumer price index. Adjusted household income in 1988 in California may not be comparable to other years due to changes in the CPS.

Figure 2.2—Percentage Change in Real Adjusted Household Income, by Income Percentile, 1967–1994

income of households at the 20th percentile fell by 13 percent in California. Before recovering fully from this recession, income at the 20th percentile in California fell again by another 20 percent during the most recent recession. The income decline for households at the 10th percentile was even greater, with income plunging 15 percent and 23 percent during the two recessions.

The national distribution of adjusted household income shows the same pattern of sharp decline at the bottom during recessions. However, the decline during recessions was greater in California than in the nation as a whole, especially for low-income households, and the growth during the recovery of the 1980s was weaker in California than in the United States.

The trends depicted in Figure 2.2 can easily be misinterpreted. The figure shows that Californians at the 10th percentile in 1994 received 24 percent less income than Californians at the 10th percentile in 1967. The cross-sectional data used in this report do not track the same people over the years. The figure, therefore, does *not* show that the income of specific people at the 10th percentile declined by 24 percent. The distinction is often subtle. When we say that "the poor got poorer," we mean that the people who were poor in 1994 were poorer than the people who were poor in 1967, but not that the same people who were poor in 1967 were even poorer in 1994.[10] This interpretation issue is

---

[10]As an analogy, imagine a class of nine third-graders lined up in order of height. The height of the fifth child in the line is the median height. Now suppose that four shorter children enter the line, making the total 13. The median child is now the seventh child in the line—the child who was third in the original line. The new median height is lower than the previous median, but no child can be said to have "experienced a decline in height."

particularly important in California where there is a high degree of mobility into and out of the state.

Figure 2.2 clearly shows the widening gap between the upper (80th and 90th) and lower (10th and 20th) percentiles. The income trends displayed in Figure 2.2 demonstrate the strong relationship between business cycle conditions and the widening distribution of household income. For both California and the United States, the recessions in the early 1980s and early 1990s stand out as periods when the distribution of household income widened rapidly, with precipitous drops in income levels at the lower percentiles of the distribution and small shorter-lived declines at the upper percentiles. In California, the widening of the distribution is more substantial than in the nation, showing a larger increase in inequality.

Because of this relationship between the business cycle and income inequality, it is important to focus on years in similar points of the business cycle when describing the long-run trends in the distribution of income. Comparing the distributions of adjusted household income in 1967 and 1994, for example, is likely to exaggerate the trends in inequality growth because the economy was strong in 1967 and weak in 1994.

To avoid such distortion, Table 2.1 summarizes the trends in Figure 2.2 for selected years at similar points in the business cycle. The first row of the table shows the absolute decline of adjusted household income for the lower-middle of the distribution (the 20th percentile) in California. Between the two major business cycle peaks spanned by our study, 1969 and 1989, the income level of households at the 20th percentile declined by 5 percent. The median of household income grew 16 percent over

Table 2.1

**Percentage Change in Real Adjusted Household Income Between
Selected Years, by Income Percentile: CPS**

	Business Cycle Peaks			Recessions
	1969–1979	1979–1989	1969–1989	1976–1994
California				
20th	2	–6	–5	–22
Median	14	2	16	–3
80th	20	5	26	15
Change in 80/20				
ratio (%)	+18	+12	+32	+48
United States				
20th	10	1	11	–1
Median	18	8	27	8
80th	22	14	38	21
Change in 80/20				
ratio (%)	+10	+13	+24	+22

SOURCE: Based on authors' calculations from the March CPS.

NOTES: Statistics reported in this table are sensitive to the consumer price index, except for the 80/20 ratio. In this and following tables the percentage change between 1969 and 1989 is not equal to the sum of the changes between 1969–1979 and 1979–1989, because the change over the 1980s is calculated from the base year of 1979 and not 1969. For example, if income grew 100 percent between 1969 and 1979 from $10 to $20, and then grew by another 100 percent between 1979 and 1989 to $40, the overall change from 1969 to 1989 would be 400, not 200, percent.

the same period. For the upper-middle of the distribution (the 80th percentile), household income grew 26 percent. Even over the 1980s, household income grew more in the United States than in California at each of these percentiles.

The widening of the distribution of adjusted household income described in Figure 2.2 can be summarized by the ratio of income at the top of the distribution to income at the bottom. The ratio of the income of the 90th percentile to the income of the 10th percentile, the 90/10 ratio, is often used as a measure of inequality. We use the 80/20 ratio instead, in order to focus on the widening of the middle of the distribution.

Table 2.1 illustrates how seriously inequality has grown in California and the nation: The 80/20 ratio increased by 32 percent in California and by 24 percent in the United States between 1969 and 1989. The 80/20 ratios in Table 2.1 suggest that California had much faster growth in inequality than the nation during the 1970s. However, as the next section will show, this finding is not confirmed by other measures of inequality that take into account the entire distribution.

This study emphasizes trends in the income distribution up until 1989 because it is impossible to determine whether later changes reflect short-run fluctuations due to the severity of the recent recession or a continuing trend of rapidly rising inequality. Nevertheless, changes between 1976 and 1994 are reported to demonstrate how seriously a deep recession, like the one of the early 1990s, can affect income inequality. As the fourth column in Table 2.1 displays, incorporating the most recent recession reflects the same pattern of income growth as shown up until 1989, but an even bleaker picture emerges, especially in California.

Other Summary Measures Also Show Rising Inequality

The percentile graphs in the previous section show the widening of the distribution of adjusted household income relative to 1967, but they do not provide an absolute measure of income inequality that would allow us to compare inequality in California and the nation. Since summary measures describe inequality with a single statistic, they make it possible to rank the level of inequality in two different distributions of income (e.g., in the United States and in California). Moreover, the summary measures used in this report are independent of the consumer price index. Even if the consumer price index overstates inflation, the magnitude of the reported summary measures is not affected.

The 80/20 ratio reported in the previous section is one summary measure of income inequality, but it suffers from the drawback that it evaluates only two positions in the distribution. There are numerous summary measures of income inequality that evaluate income throughout the distribution, including the extreme top and bottom. This study reports four commonly used and easily calculated measures: the coefficient of variation (CV), Theil's entropy (ENTROPY), mean log-deviation (MLD), and the variance of the natural logarithm of income (VLN).[11] These four were chosen in part to allow for comparability with other studies, particularly Karoly's (1993) work on income inequality in the United States.

There is no *a priori* best measure of inequality. All four measures agree on what it means to have a perfectly equal society: Each measure is scaled to equal zero when all members of society have the same amount of income. However, the measures do not agree on how to quantify deviations from perfect equality. For example, the VLN is more responsive to reductions in income near the bottom of the distribution: In an economy where nine people have $10 dollars each and one person has $8, the VLN measure will show higher inequality than if the

---

[11]The CV is the standard deviation of income divided by the mean of income. The ENTROPY measure is the mean of $[y/\text{mean}(y) * \ln(y/\text{mean}(y))]$, where y is income. The MLD is the natural logarithm of the mean of income minus the mean of the natural logarithm of income. VLN is the variance of $\ln(y)$.

anomalous person had $12, even though the deviation is $2 in both cases. This effect reflects the idea that downward deviations from equity have more negative consequences than upward ones.

The CV treats upward and downward deviations the same—the CV measure would have the same value if the anomalous person has $8 or $12. If income grows across the distribution, but grows faster for the rich, then the CV will register a greater change in inequality than the VLN will. The MLD and ENTROPY measures emphasize the bottom of the distribution more than the CV but less than the VLN. That is, the VLN is the most responsive to changes at the bottom of the income distribution, followed by the MLD, ENTROPY, and CV, in that order.

Because summary measures respond differently to income disparity, they may produce different rankings of income distributions. It is possible to find that income inequality is higher in the United States by some measures and higher in California by others. Similarly, the summary measures may show different time trends for income inequality in California. For this reason, using several summary measures of inequality and comparing the results across measures provide a fuller picture of the trends in income inequality.

Figure 2.3 illustrates the inequality of adjusted household income in California and the United States using the four measures of inequality. Overall, the measures show that the level of household income inequality in California was quite similar to that of the nation until the late 1980s. In both California and the United States, the main patterns in income inequality are consistent with a rapid rise in inequality during recession periods. The recession of the early 1980s was a period of dramatic increase in houschold incquality in both California and the nation:

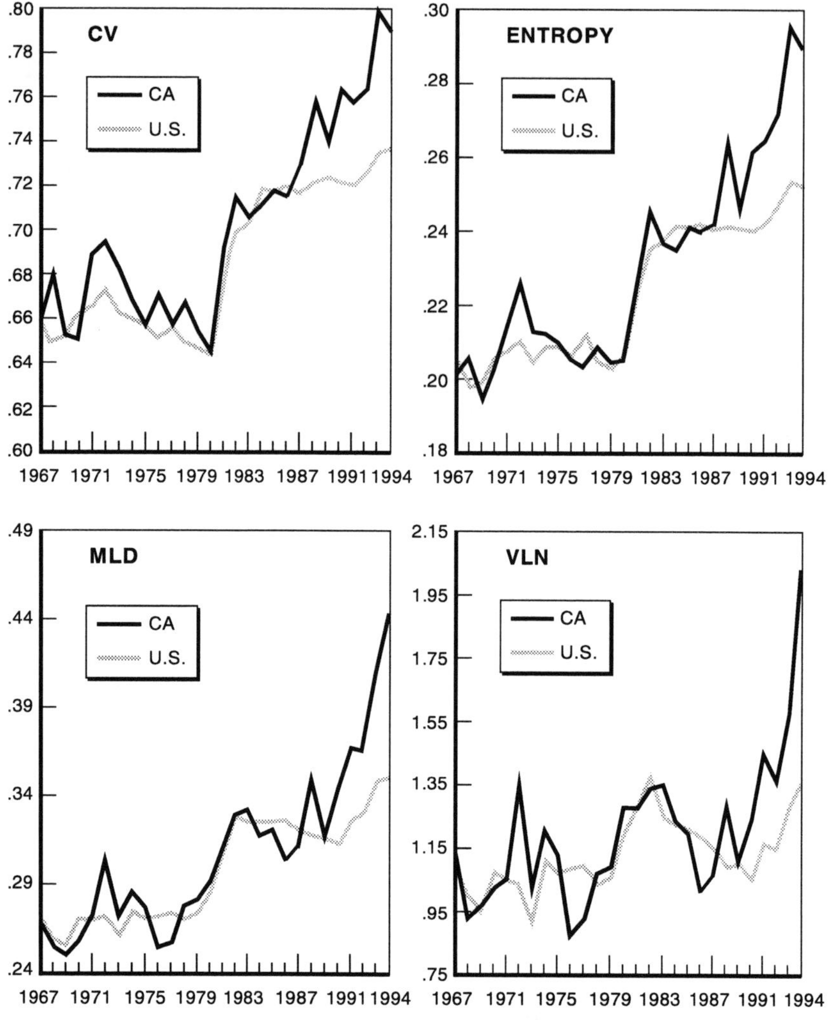

SOURCE: Based on authors' calculations from the March CPS.

NOTES: Statistics reported in this figure are not sensitive to the consumer price index. Adjusted household income in 1988 in California may not be comparable to other years due to changes in the CPS.

Figure 2.3—Summary Measures of Inequality for Real Adjusted Household Income, 1967–1994

Between 1979 and 1982, the CV grew by 9 percent in California and by 8 percent in the United States. Over the same period, the VLN grew by 23 percent in California and by 29 percent in the nation, reflecting the greater sensitivity of this measure to the declining income near the bottom of the distribution.

Adjusted household income inequality in the United States began another steep increase at the beginning of the most recent recession. In California, the increase began earlier, with small increases as early as 1987 preceding more drastic increases in the early 1990s. The late 1980s and early 1990s stand out as the only period over the last three decades that California has maintained a substantially higher level of adjusted household income inequality than the United States for several consecutive years. This is consistent with the more severe decline in adjusted household income at the median and lower percentiles in California during the most recent recession, as shown in Figure 2.2.

Census Data Also Show Rising Household Income Inequality

This report focuses primarily on income data from the Current Population Survey (CPS) because its annual data provide a fuller picture of the distribution trends than the decennial Census. Furthermore, the income data in the CPS are likely to be more accurate than the income data in the Census. For example, in 1990, the Census asked respondents about eight specific types of income. In the same year, the CPS asked about more than 20 types of income.[12] Results from Census data are

---

[12]In addition, the CPS is conducted by phone by trained survey-takers whereas the Census is taken by mail. For a further discussion of these two datasets, see Appendix A.

provided here to address the concern that the CPS may not adequately represent California.[13] The Census data do in fact confirm the trends in the distribution of adjusted household income as measured by the CPS.[14]

Table 2.2, based on Census data, shows that the growth in the upper-middle of the distribution (the 80th percentile) exceeded the growth in the lower-middle of the distribution (the 20th percentile).

Table 2.2

**Percentage Change in Real Adjusted Household Income
Between Selected Years, by Income Percentile: Census**

	Business Cycle Peaks		
	1969–1979	1979–1989	1969–1989
California			
20th	5	–4	1
Median	14	0	14
80th	8	5	24
Change in 80/20			
ratio (%)	+12	+10	+24
United States			
20th	13	4	18
Median	18	8	28
80th	20	14	36
Change in 80/20			
ratio (%)	+6	+9	+15

SOURCE: Based on authors' calculations from the decennial Census.

NOTE: Statistics reported in this table are sensitive to the consumer price index, except for the 80/20 ratio.

---

[13]For further discussion of the representativeness of the CPS for California, see Appendix B.

[14]For a comparison of the income levels at each decile for the Census and CPS, see Appendix D.

The Census data also show an absolute decline in adjusted household income at the 20th percentile in California during the 1980s, but the decline is slightly smaller than measured in the CPS, as shown in Table 2.1. Like those calculated from the CPS, the 80/20 ratios show that the widening of the distribution was more pronounced in California than it was in the United States.

Table 2.3 shows the levels and trends in the CV using the Census and the CPS. Both datasets show similar levels of adjusted household income inequality in California and the nation and a greater upward trend in inequality in California. The most significant difference between the datasets is that the Census suggests that inequality increased between 1969 and 1979 in California, whereas the CPS data indicate that the increase began after 1979.

Table 2.3

**Levels and Trends in the Coefficient of Variation for
Adjusted Household Income: CPS and Census**

	California		United States	
	CPS	Census	CPS	Census
CV: Level				
1969	0.65	0.66	0.65	0.67
1979	0.65	0.70	0.64	0.66
1989	0.74	0.75	0.72	0.73
CV: Percent change				
1969–1979	0	5	–1	–1
1979–1989	13	8	12	11
1969–1989	13	13	11	9

SOURCE: Based on authors' calculations from the March CPS and the decennial census.

NOTE: Statistics reported in this table are not sensitive to the consumer price index.

Household Income Inequality Rose Faster in California Than in Other Regions and States

The large sample size of the Census allows for measurement of income inequality at the state level, even for small states. In 1969, 20 states had higher adjusted household income inequality than California did, as measured by the CV. By 1989, California was the sixth highest state. Over the period 1969 to 1989, only Michigan experienced higher percentage growth than California in adjusted household income inequality (see Appendix D for full state rankings).

A limitation of the Census data is that they cannot be used to measure the dramatic increase in California income inequality that occurred during the deep recession of the early 1990s. Fortunately, data for the CPS do cover this period. Because of sample-size limitations, however, the CPS data can only be used to compare California to regions, not to other states.

Relative to the other regions of the country, California has experienced higher growth in adjusted household income inequality since 1969. Table 2.4 reports trends in the level and growth of the CV for ten regions of the country: California plus nine geographically defined regions (California is also included as part of the Pacific region).[15] The

---

[15]The nine Census regions are New England (Maine, New Hampshire, Vermont, Massachusetts, Rhode Island, Connecticut); Middle Atlantic (New York, New Jersey, Pennsylvania); East North Central (Ohio, Indiana, Illinois, Michigan, Wisconsin); West North Central (Minnesota, Iowa, Missouri, North Dakota, South Dakota, Nebraska, Kansas); South Atlantic (Delaware, Maryland, District of Columbia, Virginia, West Virginia, North Carolina, South Carolina, Georgia, Florida); East South Central (Kentucky, Tennessee, Alabama, Mississippi); West South Central (Arkansas, Louisiana, Oklahoma, Texas); Mountain (Montana, Idaho, Wyoming, Colorado, New Mexico, Arizona, Utah, Nevada); and Pacific (Washington, Oregon, California, Alaska, Hawaii).

Table 2.4

**Regional Trends in the Coefficient of Variation for Real Adjusted
Household Income, 1969–1994**

Region	CV *(Rank)*				Percentage Change in CV *(Rank)*		
	1969	1979	1989	1994	1969–1979	1979–1989	1989–1994
California	0.65	0.65	0.74	0.79	0	13	7
	(4)	*(4)*	*(3)*	*(1)*	*(4)*	*(2)*	*(1)*
New England	0.55	0.60	0.64	0.68	10	6	6
	(10)	*(10)*	*(10)*	*(10)*	*(1)*	*(10)*	*(2)*
Mid Atlantic	0.64	0.63	0.71	0.74	–2	13	3
	(6)	*(7)*	*(6)*	*(5)*	*(8)*	*(1)*	*(4)*
E. N. Central	0.59	0.60	0.67	0.69	1	12	3
	(9)	*(9)*	*(9)*	*(8)*	*(3)*	*(5)*	*(5)*
W. N. Central	0.62	0.61	0.67	0.68	–2	11	0
	(8)	*(8)*	*(8)*	*(9)*	*(9)*	*(7)*	*(9)*
S. Atlantic	0.67	0.66	0.72	0.73	–1	9	0
	(3)	*(3)*	*(4)*	*(6)*	*(7)*	*(9)*	*(8)*
E. S. Central	0.72	0.67	0.75	0.74	–6	11	–1
	(1)	*(2)*	*(2)*	*(4)*	*(10)*	*(8)*	*(10)*
W. S. Central	0.69	0.69	0.78	0.78	0	13	0
	(2)	*(1)*	*(1)*	*(2)*	*(5)*	*(3)*	*(7)*
Mountain	0.62	0.63	0.71	0.72	2	12	2
	(7)	*(6)*	*(7)*	*(7)*	*(2)*	*(6)*	*(6)*
Pacific	0.65	0.64	0.72	0.76	–1	12	6
	(5)	*(5)*	*(5)*	*(3)*	*(6)*	*(4)*	*(3)*

SOURCE: Based on authors' calculations from the March CPS.

NOTE: Statistics reported in this table are not sensitive to the consumer price
index.

size of California makes it reasonable to consider the state as its own
region: California has more residents than do half of the nine regions.

In 1969, California had the fourth-highest level of income inequality
of the ten regions. Between 1979 and 1989, California had the second-
highest level of growth in income inequality; between 1989 and 1994,
California had the highest. In 1994, California had the highest level of
inequality of adjusted household income of the ten regions.

Adjusted Family Income Shows Rising Inequality

Thus far, we have focused on the distribution trends in adjusted *household* income among persons. Focusing on household income implicitly assumes income-sharing among household residents regardless of relationship. Many researchers examine the distribution of *family* income rather than household income. For completeness, we also examined the trends in the distribution of adjusted family income among persons, implicitly assuming that there is no income-sharing among residents of the same household who are not related by blood, marriage, or adoption.[16] As shown below, the trend in the distribution of family income exhibits the same widening as the distribution of household income, but the rise in inequality is even more pronounced for adjusted family income.

The Census Bureau defines a "family" as the head of household and at least one resident relative: single people living alone and subfamilies unrelated to their household head are not included in the Census Bureau's sample of families. We use a more comprehensive definition: Single persons living alone are included as their own family; people who do not live alone but are not related to the head of their household are included as separate families.[17] This comprehensive definition is preferred to the Census Bureau definition because it includes the entire sample population.[18]

---

[16]Karoly and Burtless (1995) suggest an alternative to this assumption: an adjustment for family size that also allows for some sharing among residents of the same household who are not related.

[17]Separate family-level observations are constructed for each single person and for each secondary family within a household.

[18]See Appendix C for distribution trends using the Census Bureau definition of primary family.

Table 2.5 shows the change in income levels at the 20th, median, and 80th percentiles of the distribution of adjusted family income among persons. Adjusted family income at the 20th percentile fell 11 percent in California between 1969 and 1989. During the same period, income grew by 12 percent at the median and by 24 percent at the 80th percentile. This widening of the distribution led to a 39 percent increase in the 80/20 ratio over the period. In the nation, family income growth was higher at each percentile and the 80/20 ratio increased by 27 percent. Relative to the results for adjusted household income, the growth in the 80/20 ratio for adjusted family income is higher in every period.

Figure 2.4 illustrates the rise in inequality for adjusted family income, using the four summary measures discussed above. Adjusted

Table 2.5

Percentage Change in Real Adjusted Family Income Between Selected Years, by Income Percentile

	Business Cycle Peaks			Recessions
	1969–1979	1979–1989	1969–1989	1976–1994
California				
20th	–2	–9	–11	–27
Median	10	1	12	–7
80th	18	5	24	14
Change in 80/20 ratio (%)	+20	+16	+39	+56
United States				
20th	8	–1	7	–6
Median	17	7	25	7
80th	21	13	36	19
Change in 80/20 ratio (%)	+11	+14	+27	+26

SOURCE: Based on authors' calculations from the March CPS.
NOTE: Statistics reported in this table are sensitive to the consumer price index, except for the 80/20 ratio.

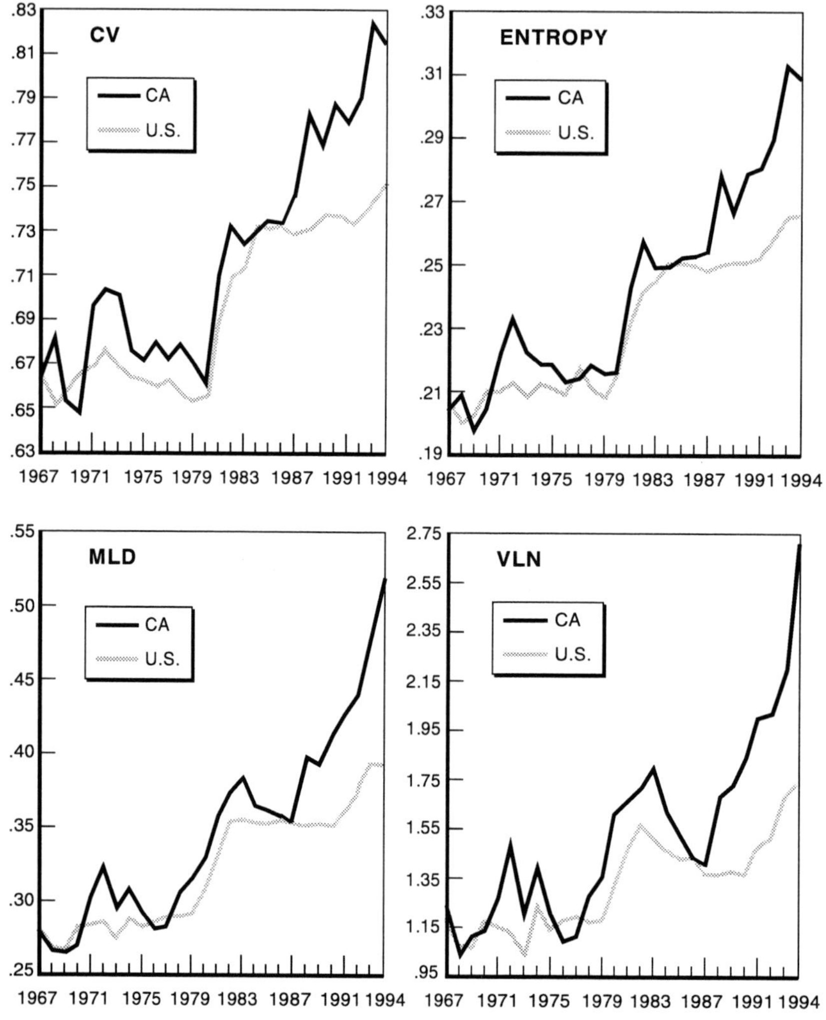

SOURCE: Based on authors' calculations from the March CPS.

NOTES: Statistics reported in this figure are not sensitive to the consumer price index. Adjusted family income in 1988 in California may not be comparable to other years due to changes in the CPS.

Figure 2.4—Summary Measures of Inequality for Real Adjusted Family Income, 1967–1994

family income inequality exhibits many of the same trends as does adjusted household income inequality. Inequality has increased in both California and the nation since the recession of the early 1980s. Inequality has increased more rapidly in the state than in the nation since the late 1980s, but the faster growth of inequality in California began even earlier for family income than for household income. Levels of adjusted family income inequality were similar to those of adjusted household income inequality in the late 1960s. By the 1990s, measures of inequality were considerably higher for families than for households, especially using those measures that emphasize income at the bottom of the distribution.

3. Trends in the Distribution of Labor Income

This chapter examines trends in the distribution of labor income, the largest component of household income. There are a number of reasons for looking at labor income inequality as well as household income inequality. Trends in adjusted household income inequality are complicated by societal changes in family size and marriage behavior.[1] In contrast, labor income inequality measures the disparity of income of *individuals* rather than families, and it is not directly affected by changes in household structure. While adjusted household income may be a better indicator of general economic well-being, labor income provides a clearer picture of changes in the economy.

---

[1] The increase in female-headed households has affected the distribution of adjusted household income, as have the falling marriage rates for men. In the past, the wives of low-income men were more likely to have earnings than the wives of high-income men. In recent years, there has been an increase in the number of families with two professional-level salary earners. The increasing correlation of husbands' and wives' earnings also has affected the distribution of adjusted household income.

As measured by annual earnings and hourly wages, the trends in labor income reveal many of the same patterns found for household income. Since the early 1980s, both California and the nation have experienced growth in labor income inequality. This result holds true for multiple definitions of labor income and measures of inequality. As was true for household income, the rising inequality of male annual earnings began in the early 1970s. In contrast, the inequality of female annual earnings declined substantially during that decade and did not begin to rise until the early 1980s.

Since 1975, male hourly wages at the top of the distribution have shown slow growth. For low-wage male workers, hourly wages have declined considerably. For female workers, in contrast, hourly wages have grown near the top of the distribution. Near the bottom of the distribution, female wages declined by a small amount in California and grew by a small amount in the nation.

What Is Labor Income?

Labor income is income from work. Labor income comprises income from wages, salary, self-employment, and one's own farm. For people who receive income from their own farm or from self-employment, however, reports of "earnings" often include income from previous capital investments such as ownership of the farm or business.[2] This income from capital is not part of labor income. Therefore, the data sample used to study labor income excludes workers who report that

---

[2]For example, a restaurant owner might show higher net income if she owns, rather than rents, her stoves.

their *primary* occupation was "self-employed"[3] and workers who receive a substantial income from self-employment or from their own farm.[4] After making these sample exclusions, we compute annual earnings as the sum of earnings from wages and salaries plus income from self-employment and farms.

To ensure that the findings do not depend on sample exclusions, we compare these results to distribution trends for total earnings among all adult workers regardless of self-employment or farm owner status. We also measure the trends in the distribution of income from wages and salary for all adults with income from these sources. Finally, we examine trends for a subsample of workers between ages 18 and 55 to remove any effects of early retirement. As is customary, all samples are limited to civilians age 18 and older who are not students and who report some earnings.[5]

The data on annual earnings include only pre-tax monetary compensation. A brief discussion of the effect of non-monetary

---

[3]People who are self-employed in incorporated businesses are not identified in the CPS before 1975. To maintain the same sample definition throughout all years, these people are not excluded from the sample in any year.

[4]The sample excludes people who report more income from their farm or business than from wages and salaries and excludes any person reporting an absolute value of more than $2,000 in income in 1994 dollars from their own farm or self-employment. Some wage and salary workers included in the sample receive a small amount of income from farms and self-employment. This income was included in annual earnings to improve estimates of hourly wages, because estimates of annual hours of work include hours worked in the farm or business. The measure of annual earnings used in this study is similar to that of Karoly (1993). Although both studies exclude people who classify themselves as "self-employed," our study additionally excludes people who receive substantial income from self-employment or farms. Also, Karoly does not include even small amounts of income from farms or self-employment in annual earnings. The results reported here for the nation are similar to those of Karoly.

[5]The sample also excludes people who report that their primary position was "without pay."

compensation and taxes on the distribution of income can be found in Appendix C.

In this chapter, we evaluate trends in both annual earnings and hourly wages. Neither measure by itself allows for a complete understanding of changes in labor income inequality: The distribution of hourly wages gives little indication of total annual earnings; the distribution of annual earnings is confounded by differences in hours of work. Using both of these measures, along with household income as discussed in the previous chapter, provides a more complete picture of income inequality in California.

We examine the trends in income inequality for male and female workers separately because of the recent significant changes in the labor force participation of women. Over the years of the study, women's labor force participation rate has increased from 51 percent to 61 percent in California; between 1975 and 1994, the average hours worked per year among adult women in the labor force increased from 780 to 980.[6]

Trends in the Distribution of Labor Income Among Males

Inequality in male annual earnings and hourly wages is rising. There has been a slow growth in annual earnings and hourly wages near the top of the distribution and a substantial decline near the bottom—and even at the median after 1986 in California. In addition, California had one

---

[6]Labor market participation rates are based on the authors' calculations from the CPS. The sample includes civilian women age 18 and older. The CPS began including information on hours of work only in 1975. Annual hours are calculated as the product of annual weeks of work and usual hours worked per week of work.

of the highest increases of any state in male annual earnings inequality between 1969 and 1989.

The Widening Distribution of Male Annual Earnings

Figure 3.1 illustrates the trends in annual earnings between 1967 and 1994 for the 10th, 20th, median, 80th, and 90th percentiles of male workers for California and the nation. The figure shows much the same pattern as observed for adjusted household income: The distribution of male annual earnings widened over the past three decades, with the most noticeable increases occurring during periods of recession in the early and mid 1970s, the early 1980s, and the early 1990s.

During each recession, male annual earnings fell drastically for the lower and lower-middle positions of the distributions in California and the nation. The decline in male annual earnings was greater in California than in the nation because of slower growth in recovery periods and more rapid decline in the recessions of the early 1970s and early 1990s. For example, in California, men at the 20th percentile in 1971 had 16 percent lower annual earnings than men at the 20th percentile in 1969. For the nation, the decline was 8 percent. The recession of the early 1990s hit California even harder. Between 1989 and 1993, the 20th percentile fell 14 percent in the nation but 27 percent in California.

While the trends in the distribution of male earnings are similar to those of adjusted household income in their overall shape, male earnings exhibit much slower growth. Table 3.1 summarizes the trends in male earnings for comparable years in the business cycle. The 80th percentile

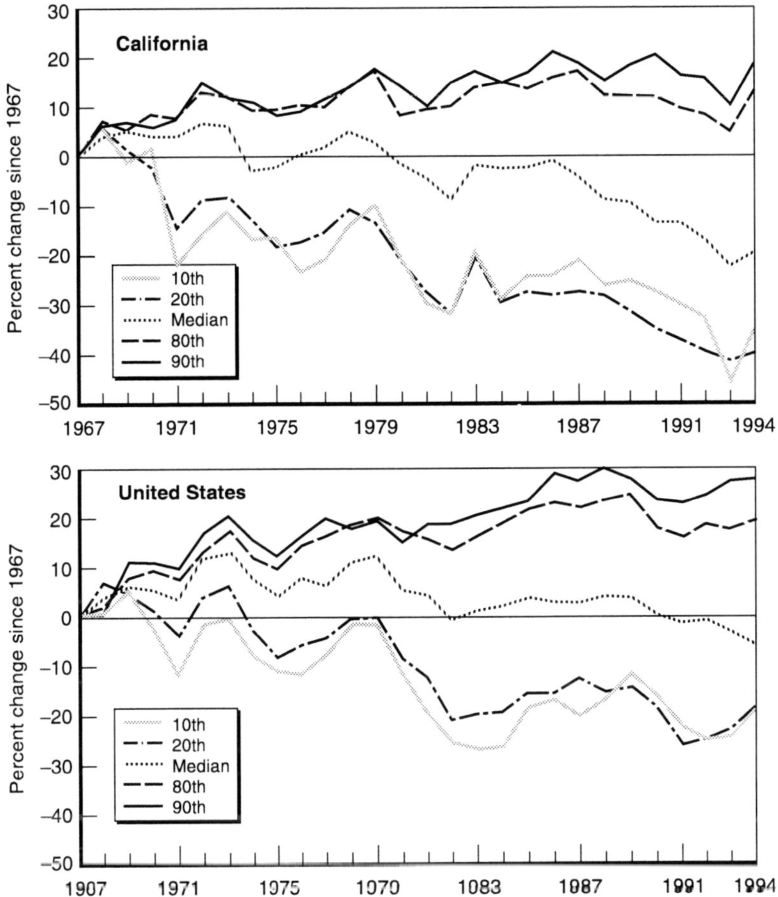

SOURCE: Based on authors' calculations from the March CPS.

NOTES: Sample includes civilians age 18 and older who received wage and salary income. Sample excludes students, those self-employed who are not in incorporated businesses, workers whose primary position is unpaid, workers who receive more farm or self-employment income than wage and salary income, and workers who receive more than $2,000 (real 1994 dollars) from farm or self-employment income. Annual earnings are computed as the sum of earnings from wages, salaries, self-employment and farms. Statistics reported in this figure are sensitive to the consumer price index. Real annual earnings in 1988 in California may not be comparable to other years due to changes in the CPS.

Figure 3.1—Percentage Change in Real Annual Earnings for Males, by Income Percentile, 1967–1994

Table 3.1

**Percentage Change in Real Annual Earnings for Males
Between Selected Years, by Income Percentile: CPS**

	Business Cycle Peaks			Recessions
	1969–1979	1979–1989	1969–1989	1976–1994
California				
20th	–15	–21	–33	–27
Median	–2	–12	–13	–20
80th	11	–5	6	2
Change in 80/20				
ratio (%)	+30	+21	+57	+41
United States				
20th	–4	–14	–18	–14
Median	5	–7	–2	–13
80th	11	4	16	4
Change in 80/20				
ratio (%)	+16	+22	+42	+21

SOURCE: Based on authors' calculations from the March CPS.

NOTES: See the notes to Figure 3.1 for sample criteria and the calculation of annual earnings. Statistics reported in this table are sensitive to the consumer price index, except for the 80/20 ratio.

of male earnings climbed only 6 percent in California between 1969 and 1989, in contrast with a 26 percent growth in adjusted household income.

After 1979, the nation displayed a decline in the median of male earnings, particularly during recessions. The median in California fell throughout the period of the study, dropping 13 percent between 1969 and 1989. Surprisingly, the most recent decline in median male earnings began as early as 1987 in California, three years before the most recent recession.

Despite the slow growth at the top of the distribution of male annual earnings in California, the 80/20 ratio increased a staggering 57 percent between 1969 and 1989 because of the drastic decline in earnings at the

20th percentile. The national 80/20 ratio also shows a remarkable (though smaller) increase of 42 percent.

Summary Measures Show Rising Inequality in Male Annual Earnings

As Figure 3.2 shows, the summary measures of inequality (introduced in Chapter 2) demonstrate the increasing trend in male annual earnings inequality over the last three decades. Male annual earnings show a clear pattern: Inequality rose sharply during recessions and remained at new, higher levels during recovery periods. In many cases, in fact, inequality continued to increase even during periods of growth.[7]

Beginning in the 1970s, male earnings inequality was consistently higher in California than in the nation, except for a brief period in the mid 1980s. The measures show that the gap between California and the United States began to widen noticeably as early as 1987. Although inequality did increase in the nation during the most recent recession, levels of inequality in California continue to be considerably higher.

Census Data Show Rising Inequality of Male Annual Earnings

The Census results, shown in Table 3.2, confirm the large decline in earnings near the bottom of the distribution and the slow growth in

---

[7]All four measures (and especially the VLN) appear to show a decrease in inequality in the early 1980s because of the large spike in inequality between 1979 and 1982. The cause of this spike is clear in Figure 3.1: Earnings fell sharply for the bottom of the distribution between 1979 and 1982 and then showed some compensating recovery in the next few years. If the spike is ignored, the continuing upward pattern of increasing inequality is clear.

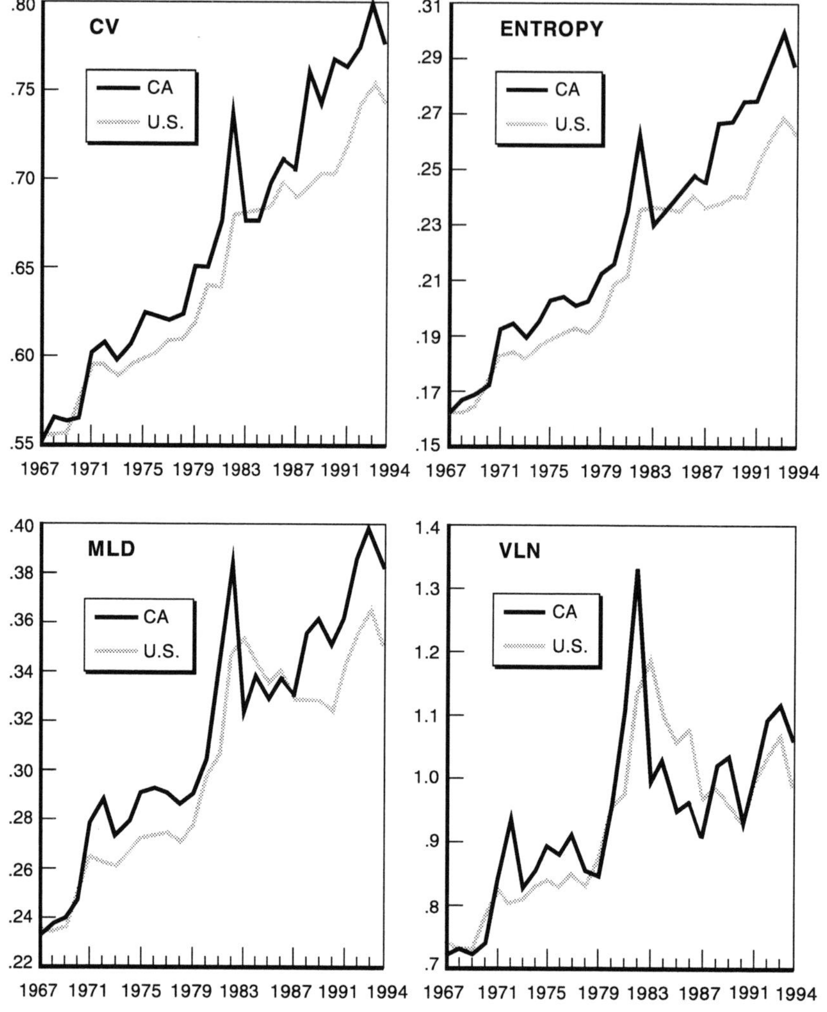

SOURCE: Based on authors' calculations from the March CPS.

NOTES: See the notes to Figure 3.1 for sample criteria and calculation of annual earnings. Statistics reported in this figure are not sensitive to the consumer price index. Real annual earnings in 1988 in California may not be comparable to other years due to changes in the CPS.

Figure 3.2—Summary Measures of Inequality for Male Annual Earnings, 1967–1994

Table 3.2

**Percentage Change in Real Annual Earnings for Males,
by Income Percentile: Census**

	Annual Earnings		
	1969–1979	1979–1989	1969–1989
California			
20th	–18	–18	–33
Median	–3	–12	–14
80th	10	–7	3
Change in 80/20			
ratio (%)	+35	+13	+53
United States			
20th	–6	–9	–14
Median	6	–9	–4
80th	11	–1	9
Change in 80/20			
ratio (%)	+18	+8	+28

SOURCE: Based on authors' calculations from the decennial Census.

NOTES: See the notes to Figure 3.1 for sample criteria and the calculation of annual earnings. Statistics reported in this table are sensitive to the consumer price index, except for the 80/20 ratio.

earnings near the top found by the CPS. The main difference between the Census and CPS results is that over the period 1969 to 1989, the national 80/20 ratio increased by 28 percent according to the Census and by 42 percent according to the CPS. For California, the results are closer: a 53 percent increase according to the Census and a 57 percent increase according to the CPS.

The Census data show slower growth but higher levels of inequality. For example, the coefficient of variation for male annual earnings was 0.63 in California in 1969 as calculated from the Census (see Table 3.3).

Table 3.3

Levels and Trends in the Coefficient of Variation for Male Annual Earnings: CPS and Census

	California		United States	
	CPS	Census	CPS	Census
CV: Level				
1969	0.56	0.63	0.56	0.63
1979	0.65	0.72	0.62	0.68
1989	0.75	0.76	0.70	0.71
CV: Percent change				
1969–1979	15	14	11	9
1979–1989	14	5	13	4
1969–1989	32	20	26	14

SOURCE: Based on authors' calculations from the March CPS and the decennial Census.

NOTES: See the notes to Figure 3.1 for sample criteria and the calculation of annual earnings. Statistics reported in this table are not sensitive to the consumer price index.

For that same year, the CV calculated from the CPS was 0.56. Despite these differences, both datasets show a substantial rise in inequality in California that exceeded the rise in the United States.

The Widening Distribution of Male Hourly Wages

We examine trends in hourly wages, in addition to annual earnings, to observe changes in salary separate from changes in hours worked. Hourly wages are calculated by dividing annual earnings by annual hours; annual hours are the product of weeks worked and usual hours worked per week of work.[8] Figure 3.3 shows the widening distribution

---

[8]Hourly wages are measured imprecisely because they are calculated from annual data. This imprecision leads to extreme values in some years (e.g., some years have several observations with an hourly wage of less than $1). To avoid fluctuation in the summary measures of inequality due to extreme values, hourly wages were top-coded at 97 percent and bottom-coded at 3 percent in all years.

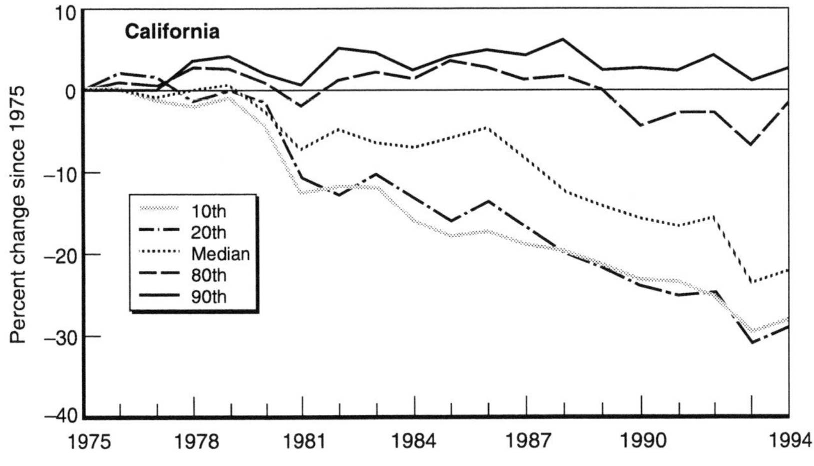

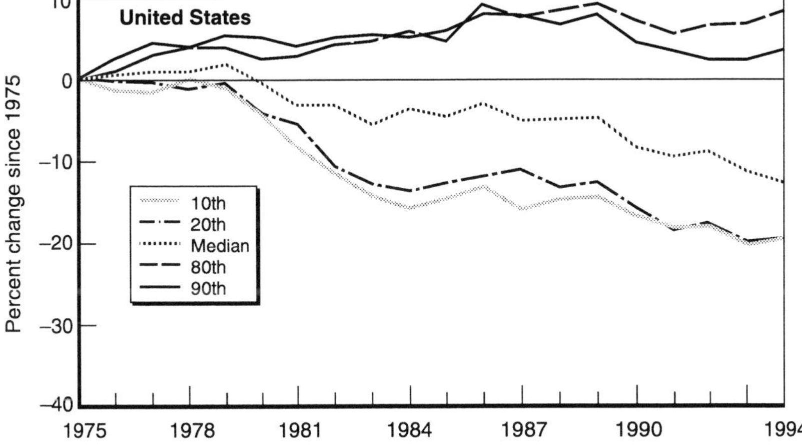

SOURCE: Based on authors' calculations from the March CPS.

NOTES: Hourly wage is calculated as annual earnings divided by the product of annual weeks of work and usual hours worked per week of work. Hourly wage is not available before 1975 in the March CPS. See notes to Figure 3.1 for sample criteria and calculation of annual earnings. Statistics reported in this figure are sensitive to the consumer price index. Real hourly wages in 1988 in California may not be comparable to other years due to changes in the CPS.

Figure 3.3—Percentage Change in Real Hourly Wages for Males, by Income Percentile, 1975–1994

of male hourly wages. (The figure begins in 1975 because information on hours worked per week is not available in earlier years of the CPS.[9])

The most striking features of Figure 3.3 are the slow growth at the top and the decline at the bottom of the distribution of male hourly wages in both California and the United States. Over most of the period, inequality increased even though wages at the 90th percentile were never more than 10 percent higher than they had been in 1975.

Table 3.4 summarizes these trends. Between 1979 and 1989 in California, male hourly wages fell by 21 percent at the 20th percentile and fell by 14 percent at the median. Even at the 80th percentile, wages fell 2 percent. The nation exhibited a similar pattern but with smaller declines. Because of the faster decline in wages at the 20th percentile in California, the 80/20 ratio increased by 24 percent in the state compared to 17 percent in the nation.

Summary Measures Show Rising Inequality in Male Wages

The summary measures of inequality shown in Figure 3.4 confirm that male wage inequality has risen steadily and significantly in California since 1977. As with male earnings inequality, male hourly wage inequality was higher in California than in the nation for most of the years of the study. Since the late 1980s, however, male wage inequality

---

[9]Before the 1976 survey, the CPS did not ask about hours of work in a usual week in the previous year. This information is needed to calculate hourly wages from annual earnings in the previous year. Hourly wages were not computed from the Census data because the 1970 Census survey did not ask about hours of work per week in the previous year.

Table 3.4

Percentage Change in Real Hourly Wages for Males
Between Selected Years, by Income Percentile

	Business Cycle Peaks	Recessions
	1979–1989	1976–1994
California		
20th	–21	–30
Median	–14	–22
80th	–2	–2
Change in 80/20		
ratio (%)	+24	+40
United States		
20th	–12	–19
Median	–6	–13
80th	3	1
Change in 80/20		
ratio (%)	+17	+25

SOURCE: Based on authors' calculations from the March CPS.

NOTES: Hourly wage is calculated as annual earnings divided by the product of annual weeks of work and usual hours worked per week of work. Hourly wage is not available before 1975 in the March CPS. See the notes to Figure 3.1 for sample criteria and the calculation of annual earnings. Statistics reported in this table are sensitive to the consumer price index, except for the 80/20 ratio.

grew more rapidly in California, widening the difference in inequality between California and the nation.

Male Labor Income Inequality Rose Faster in California Than in Other Regions and States

Relative to the other regions of the country, California experienced high growth in male hourly wage inequality. Table 3.5 shows the CV for

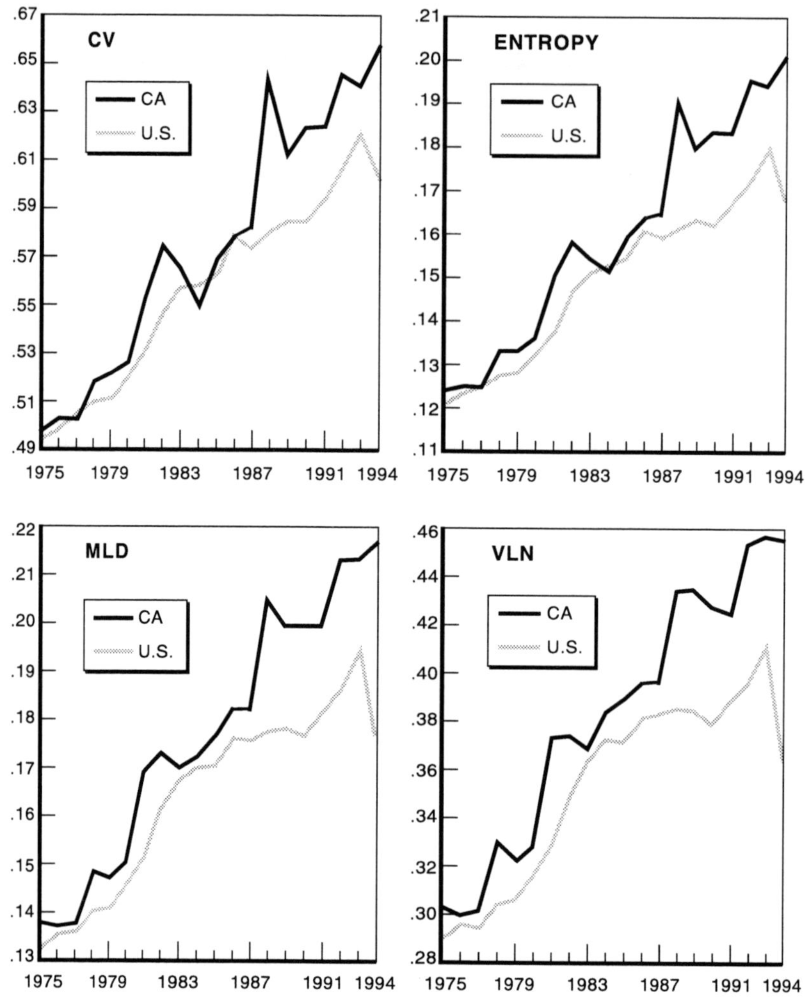

SOURCE: Based on authors' calculations from the March CPS.

NOTES: Hourly wage is calculated as annual earnings divided by the product of annual weeks of work and usual hours worked per week of work. Hourly wage is not available before 1975 in the March CPS. See the notes to Figure 3.1 for sample criteria and calculation of annual earnings. Statistics reported in this figure are not sensitive to the consumer price index. Real hourly wages in 1988 in California may not be comparable to other years due to changes in the CPS.

Figure 3.4—Summary Measures of Inequality for Male Hourly Wages, 1975–1994

Table 3.5

Regional Trends in the Coefficient of Variation for Real Hourly Wages Among Males, 1979–1994

Region	CV (Rank)			Percentage Change in CV (Rank)	
	1979	1989	1994	1979–1989	1989–1994
California	0.52	0.61	0.66	18	7
	(3)	(2)	(1)	(3)	(4)
New England	0.52	0.54	0.56	5	3
	(6)	(9)	(10)	(10)	(8)
Mid Atlantic	0.48	0.57	0.60	18	6
	(9)	(6)	(5)	(1)	(5)
E. N. Central	0.45	0.53	0.58	18	10
	(10)	(10)	(8)	(2)	(1)
W. N. Central	0.50	0.57	0.57	14	1
	(8)	(7)	(9)	(6)	(10)
S. Atlantic	0.54	0.58	0.63	8	8
	(1)	(4)	(4)	(9)	(3)
E. S. Central	0.52	0.57	0.60	10	5
	(4)	(5)	(6)	(7)	(6)
W. S. Central	0.54	0.63	0.64	16	2
	(2)	(1)	(2)	(4)	(9)
Mountain	0.52	0.56	0.59	8	5
	(5)	(8)	(7)	(8)	(7)
Pacific	0.51	0.59	0.64	16	8
	(7)	(3)	(3)	(5)	(2)

SOURCE: Based on authors' calculations from the March CPS.

NOTES: Hourly wage is calculated as annual earnings divided by the product of annual weeks of work and usual hours worked per week of work. Hourly wage is not available before 1975 in the March CPS. See the notes to Figure 3.1 for sample criteria and the calculation of annual earnings. Statistics reported in this table are not sensitive to the consumer price index.

California and the nine geographic regions, including California's own Pacific region. In 1979, the CV of male hourly wages in California was the third-highest among the ten regions; in 1989, it was second; by

1994, inequality was higher in California than in any other region.[10] Appendix D presents the same analysis for male annual earnings.

Comparing male annual earnings trends between the states further emphasizes the growth in inequality in California. The Census data show that 20 states had greater inequality than California in 1969, as measured by the CV. Between 1969 and 1989, California was tied with Indiana and Ohio for the fastest percentage growth in male earnings inequality in the country. In 1989, only two states had higher levels of male earnings inequality. Appendix D reports the CV for all 50 states in 1969 and 1989.

Other Definitions of Male Labor Income Show Rising Inequality

The labor income results reported in the previous sections are based on a data sample that excludes workers who are primarily self-employed or farm owners. This sample definition is preferable because of the difficulty in separating capital income from labor income for people who work in their own business or farm. However, including these workers and looking at the sum of income from wages, salary, self-employment, and farms does not alter the basic trends of decline near the bottom of the distribution, slow growth near the top, and rising inequality. For California between 1969 and 1989, the decline in male annual earnings at the 20th percentile was 30 percent among all workers, compared to 33 percent in the restricted sample of wage and salary workers (shown in Table 3.1). The growth in male earnings at the 80th percentile was about

---

[10]This result is consistent with the regional inequality trends found by Karoly and Klerman (1994).

5 percent in both samples. Over the same period, the growth in the CV was 25 percent for all workers and 32 percent for wage and salary workers.

The same general trends also hold for the distributions of hourly wages among all workers, of annual earnings and hourly wages among wage and salary workers ages 18 to 55, and of wage and salary income. See Appendix C for further details.

Trends in the Distribution of Labor Income Among Females

The trends in inequality of female annual earnings are quite different from those of male annual earnings. The distribution of female annual earnings narrowed during the 1970s, when women's incomes rose substantially near the bottom of the distribution. In the 1980s, the declining inequality of female annual earnings either slowed or reversed itself, depending on which measure of inequality is used. In contrast, all the measures show that the inequality of hourly wages among women increased during the 1980s. The difference between the trends in annual earnings and hourly wages suggests that some of the increase in female earnings, especially in the lower ranks of the distribution, was due to increased hours of work. The levels and trends of female labor income inequality, however, were nearly identical in California and the nation, even over the last decade.

The Narrowing, Then Widening, Distribution of Female Annual Earnings

In contrast to male annual earnings and adjusted household income, female annual earnings inequality actually declined between 1967 and the early 1980s. As Figure 3.5 shows, growth was fastest among women at the *bottom* of the distribution during the 1970s in both California and the nation: The upper lines on the figure represent earnings growth at the 10th and 20th percentiles. The relative gains of the lowest-earning women were short-lived, however. In the 1980s, annual earnings began to grow for women in the upper half of the distribution, and, interestingly, did not show the same tendency as male annual earnings to fall during recessions. Earnings at the lower percentiles did continue to grow but fell during recessions, especially in California.

Table 3.6 allows us to see these trends clearly. The income at the 20th percentile increased over the 1970s, growing 61 percent in

Table 3.6

**Percentage Change in Real Annual Earnings for Females
Between Selected Years, by Income Percentile**

	Business Cycle Peaks			Recessions
	1969–1979	1979–1989	1969–1989	1976–1994
California				
20th	61	13	82	15
Median	22	6	29	27
80th	10	22	35	30
Change in 80/20 ratio (%)	–31	+8	–26	+13
United States				
20th	44	20	72	43
Median	20	11	33	28
80th	16	20	39	33
Change in 80/20 ratio (%)	–20	+0	–20	–7

SOURCE: Based on authors' calculations from the March CPS.

NOTES: See the notes to Figure 3.1 for sample criteria and the calculation of annual earnings. Statistics reported in this table are sensitive to the consumer price index, except for the 80/20 ratio.

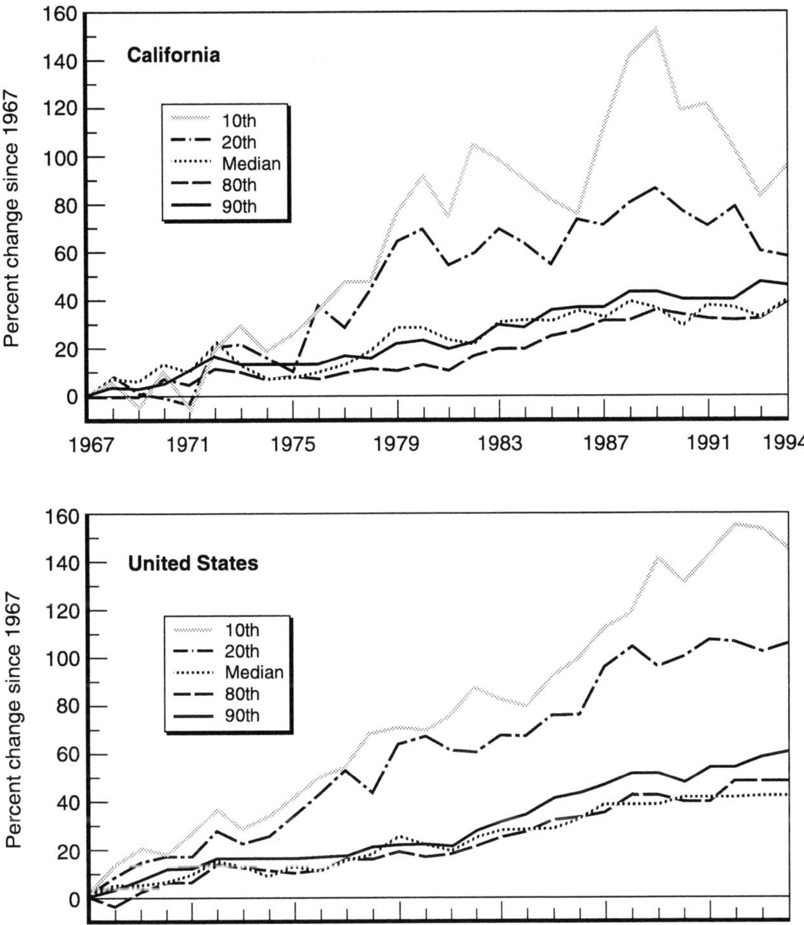

SOURCE: Based on authors' calculations from the March CPS.

NOTES: See the notes to Figure 3.1 for sample criteria and calculation of annual earnings. Statistics reported in this figure are sensitive to the consumer price index. Real annual earnings in 1988 in California may not be comparable to other years due to changes in the CPS.

Figure 3.5—Percentage Change in Real Annual Earnings for Females, by Income Percentile, 1967–1994

49

California and 44 percent in the nation. Female earnings at the 80th percentile grew at a slower pace, so that the 80/20 ratio fell by 31 percent in California and by 20 percent in the nation over that decade. In California in the 1980s, the 80th percentile grew faster than the 20th, leading to an 8 percent increase in the 80/20 ratio. In the nation, the 80/20 ratio was the same in 1989 as in 1979.

Measures of Inequality Show Falling, Then Rising, Inequality in Female Annual Earnings

The summary measures in Figure 3.6 all show that female earnings inequality fell during the 1970s and increased beginning in the early 1980s. After 1986, the trends in inequality are dependent on which measure is used. The CV shows a continuing increase throughout the 1980s, whereas the other measures exhibit fluctuations without clear trends.[11] Unlike trends in inequality for male earnings and household income, trends in female earnings inequality were virtually identical in California and the nation, even in the late 1980s. Inequality did rise more sharply in California in the early 1990s, but the difference between the state and the nation had narrowed substantially by 1994.

Census Data Show a Fall and Then a Rise in Inequality of Female Annual Earnings

Table 3.7 shows the trends in the distribution of female annual earnings calculated from the Census data. The picture of growth is

---

[11]The fact that the measures do not agree on whether inequality was higher in the 1990s than in the early 1970s reflects the tremendous growth in the income of the lowest-earning women. The two measures that put more weight on the bottom of the distribution—the MLD and the VLN—do not show as steep an increase in inequality as the other measures do.

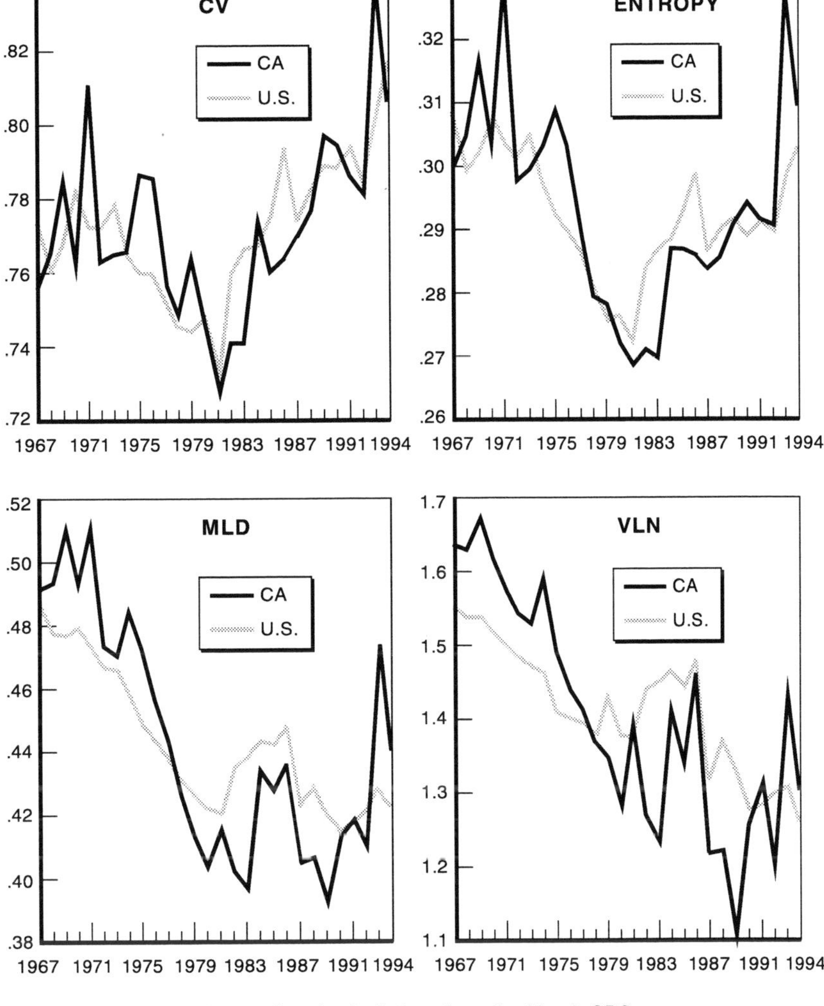

SOURCE: Based on authors' calculations from the March CPS.

NOTES: See the notes to Figure 3.1 for sample criteria and calculation of annual earnings. Statistics reported in this figure are not sensitive to the consumer price index. Real annual earnings in 1988 in California may not be comparable to other years due to changes in the CPS.

Figure 3.6—Summary Measures of Inequality for Female Annual Earnings, 1967–1994

Table 3.7

**Percentage Change in Real Annual Earnings and Hourly Wages
for Females, by Income Percentile: Census**

	Annual Earnings		
	1969–1979	1979–1989	1969–1989
California			
20th	52	13	72
Median	12	14	27
80th	9	18	29
Change in 80/20			
ratio (%)	–28	+4	–25
United States			
20th	30	22	58
Median	15	12	28
80th	11	19	33
Change in 80/20			
ratio (%)	–15	–2	–16

SOURCE: Based on authors' calculations from the decennial Census.

NOTES: See the notes to Figure 3.1 for sample criteria and the calculation of annual earnings. Statistics reported in this table are sensitive to the consumer price index, except for the 80/20 ratio.

similar to that found using the CPS, shown in Table 3.6. In California, the 80/20 ratio decreased in the 1970s and then increased by a small amount in the 1980s. The overall decline in the 80/20 ratio between 1969 and 1989 was nearly identical in the CPS and the Census (26 percent versus 25 percent for California). The Census data do not show as much growth in female earnings as the CPS data do.

Table 3.8 depicts the very similar levels of female annual earnings inequality between the CPS and the Census data, as measured by the CV. In addition, the changes in the CV are also similar—the main

Table 3.8

**Levels and Trends in the Coefficient of Variation for
Female Annual Earnings: CPS and Census**

	California		United States	
	CPS	Census	CPS	Census
CV: Level				
1969	0.78	0.77	0.77	0.77
1979	0.76	0.78	0.74	0.77
1989	0.80	0.84	0.79	0.78
CV: Percent change				
1969–1979	−3	1	−3	−1
1979–1989	4	8	6	2
1969–1989	2	9	3	1

SOURCE: Based on authors' calculations from the March CPS and the decennial Census.

NOTES: See the notes to Figure 3.1 for sample criteria and the calculation of annual earnings. Statistics reported in this table are not sensitive to the consumer price index.

difference is that the Census shows higher inequality growth in California than the CPS does.

The Widening Distribution of Female Hourly Wages

The trends in the distribution of female annual earnings reflect the increase in hours worked by women in the labor market. Among women who work, average hours increased 26 percent between 1975 and 1994 in California. Examining the trends in the distribution of hourly wages removes the effect of hours of work. These trends are portrayed in Figure 3.7.

Like the distribution of female annual earnings, the distribution of female hourly wages narrowed between 1975 and 1979 as wages for the lowest-paid women rose quickly. During the recession of the early

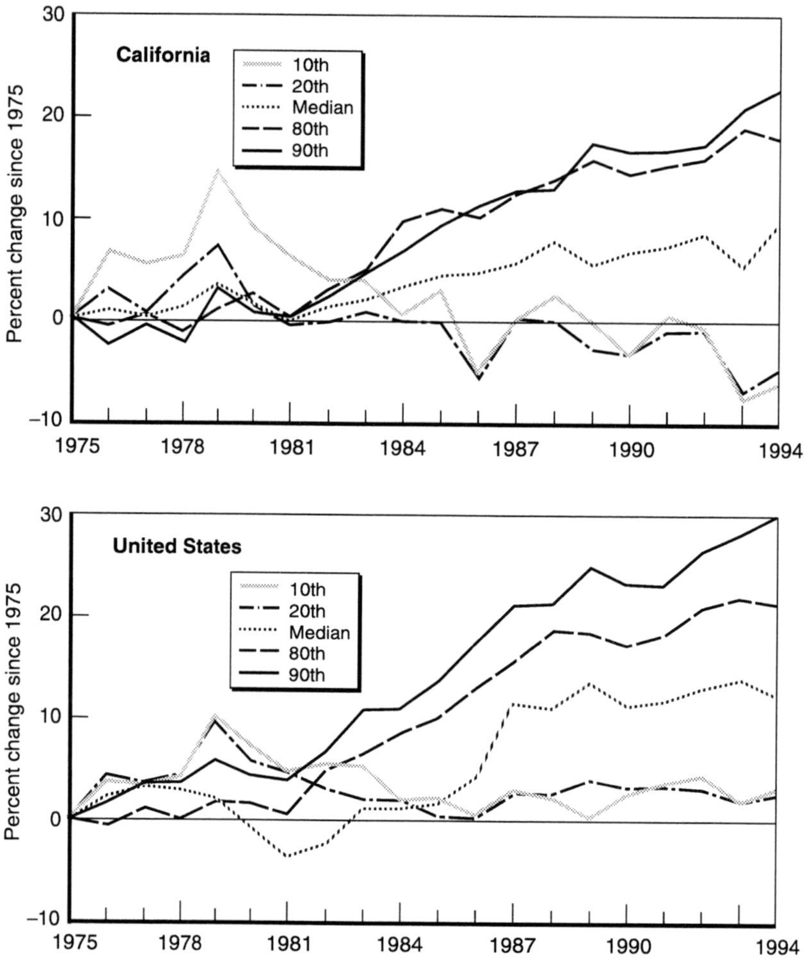

SOURCE: Based on authors' calculations from the March CPS.

NOTES: Hourly wage is calculated as annual earnings divided by the product of annual weeks of work and usual hours worked per week of work. Hourly wage is not available before 1975 in the March CPS. See the notes to Figure 3.1 for sample criteria and calculation of annual earnings. Statistics reported in this figure are sensitive to the consumer price index. Real hourly wage in 1988 in California may not be comparable to other years due to changes in the CPS.

Figure 3.7—Percentage Change in Real Hourly Wages for Females, by Income Percentile, 1975–1994

1980s, however, wages fell throughout the distribution. When female wages began to rise again, they grew in a familiar pattern: Wages grew fastest at the upper percentiles. In California, female hourly wages fell at the 10th percentile between 1985 and 1994.

In contrast to male wages, female wages near the top of the distribution in California grew over the 1980s, and even in the early 1990s. Moreover, female wages did not show the same strong influence of recessions. In addition, female wages grew only slightly faster in the nation than in California. As Table 3.9 shows, wages at the median increased by 2 percent in California and by 8 percent in the nation between 1979 and 1989. At the 20th percentile, female wages fell 9

Table 3.9

**Percentage Change in Real Hourly Wages for Females
Between Selected Years, by Income Percentile**

	Business Cycle Peaks	Recessions
	1979–1989	1976–1994
California		
20th	–9	–8
Median	2	8
80th	15	18
Change in 80/20 ratio (%)	+26	+28
United States		
20th	–5	–2
Median	8	10
80th	16	22
Change in 80/20 ratio (%)	+22	+24

SOURCE: Based on authors' calculations from the March CPS.

NOTES: Hourly wage is calculated as annual earnings divided by the product of annual weeks of work and usual hours worked per week of work. Hourly wage is not available before 1975 in the March CPS. See the notes to Figure 3.1 for sample criteria and the calculation of annual earnings. Statistics reported in this table are sensitive to the consumer price index, except for the 80/20 ratio.

percent in California compared with 5 percent in the nation over the
same period. At the upper end of the distribution, the increase was
nearly identical in California and the United States.

Measures of Inequality Show Rising Inequality in Female Hourly Wages

Female hourly wages show a clear upward trend in inequality
beginning in the early 1980s, as depicted in Figure 3.8. This is in
contrast to the results for female annual earnings, which depend on the
measure of inequality used. Like female annual earnings, hourly wage
inequality in California tracks closely with that of the nation.

Female Labor Income Inequality Is Similar in California to Other Regions and States

Table 3.10 compares female wage inequality in California and in the
regions of the country. It confirms the finding, shown in Figure 3.8,
that, in contradistinction to household and male labor income, female
wages did not show higher levels of inequality in California than in the
nation. In the business cycle peak of 1979 and in the business cycle
trough of 1994, California's level of female earnings inequality was firmly
in the middle of the regions. Even its apparent high ranking in 1989 is
somewhat misleading: Five of the regions had levels of inequality nearly
identical to California's in that year. Appendix D presents the same
analysis for female annual earnings.

Compared with other states, California had a moderate level of
female earnings inequality in 1989 (as measured by the CV)—16 states
had higher levels. However, between 1969 and 1989, 39 states
experienced larger declines in inequality than California did.

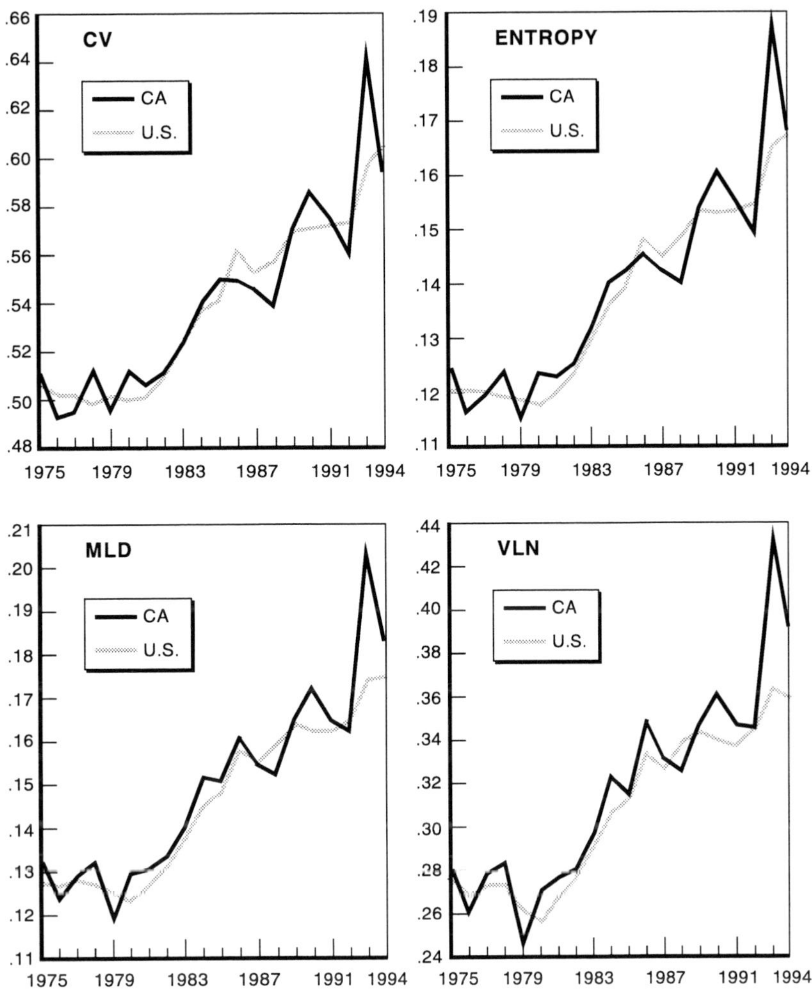

SOURCE: Based on authors' calculations from the March CPS.

NOTES: Hourly wage is calculated as annual earnings divided by the product of annual weeks of work and usual hours worked per week of work. Hourly wage is not available before 1975 in the March CPS. See the notes to Figure 3.1 for sample criteria and calculation of annual earnings. Statistics reported in this figure are not sensitive to the consumer price index. Real hourly wages in 1988 in California may not be comparable to other years due to changes in the CPS.

Figure 3.8—Summary Measures of Inequality for Female Hourly Wages, 1975–1994

Table 3.10

Regional Trends in the Coefficient of Variation for Real Hourly Wages Among Females, 1979–1994

Region	CV (Rank)			Percentage Change in CV (Rank)	
	1979	1989	1994	1979–1989	1989–1994
California	0.50	0.57	0.59	15	4
	(5)	*(2)*	*(5)*	*(3)*	*(8)*
New England	0.48	0.53	0.57	10	6
	(9)	*(10)*	*(10)*	*(9)*	*(4)*
Mid Atlantic	0.49	0.57	0.60	16	5
	(6)	*(1)*	*(2)*	*(2)*	*(5)*
E. N. Central	0.49	0.55	0.60	13	9
	(7)	*(8)*	*(4)*	*(5)*	*(3)*
W. N. Central	0.48	0.57	0.57	19	0
	(10)	*(5)*	*(9)*	*(1)*	*(10)*
S. Atlantic	0.50	0.56	0.61	12	9
	(4)	*(6)*	*(1)*	*(8)*	*(2)*
E. S. Central	0.49	0.55	0.58	14	5
	(8)	*(7)*	*(8)*	*(4)*	*(6)*
W. S. Central	0.51	0.57	0.59	12	4
	(2)	*(3)*	*(6)*	*(7)*	*(9)*
Mountain	0.55	0.54	0.60	−1	10
	(1)	*(9)*	*(3)*	*(10)*	*(1)*
Pacific	0.51	0.57	0.59	12	4
	(3)	*(4)*	*(7)*	*(6)*	*(7)*

SOURCE: Based on authors' calculations from the March CPS.

NOTES: Hourly wage is calculated as annual earnings divided by the product of annual weeks of work and usual hours worked per week of work. Hourly wage is not available before 1975 in the March CPS. See the notes to Figure 3.1 for sample criteria and the calculation of annual earnings. Statistics reported in this table are not sensitive to the consumer price index.

Other Definitions of Female Labor Income Show Falling, Then Rising, Inequality

As was true for male labor income, alternative sample definitions do not alter the basic trends in female labor income reported in the previous sections. Female annual earnings grew rapidly near the bottom of the distribution and inequality declined until the early 1980s. There is one notable difference in results between the sample of all workers and the restricted sample of wage and salary workers: Annual earnings inequality among all female workers followed an increasing trend after 1983 for all the summary measures of inequality. This is in contrast to the trends in inequality after 1983 for female wage and salary workers, which depended on the summary measure used (as shown in Figure 3.6). See Appendix C for further results using the alternative definitions of female annual earnings and hourly wages.

4. Conclusions and Implications for Policy and Future Research

Our study finds a large increase in income inequality in California over the last three decades for both household income and male earnings. This rise in income inequality is explained by a dramatic decline in income at the lower and lower-middle ranks of the distribution, and a simultaneous growth in income in the upper ranks. The trends in income inequality show a strong relationship to the business cycle: Inequality grew fastest during the recessions of the early 1970s, early 1980s, and early 1990s.

Until the late 1980s, the levels and trends in income inequality in California and the nation were similar. Since that time, inequality has grown faster in California than in the United States. Moreover, compared to the nation, California has experienced slower income growth throughout the distribution.

Provocative as these findings are, measuring the trends in the distribution of income is only the first step in understanding them and their implications for policy. As California designs programs to promote equity, it will benefit from research on the relationship between existing state policies and income inequality, as well as from a better understanding of the causes of rising inequality in the state. In addition, the income trends measured in this study provide an incomplete picture of the distribution of economic well-being. Distribution trends for more-comprehensive definitions of income (e.g., accounting for taxes and non-monetary compensation) and the issue of income variability remain to be studied.

Public Policy and the Distribution of Income

Continued growth in income inequality is not inevitable. As a society, we face a choice as to whether we will act to reverse the trend in growing income inequality. Many policy mechanisms already exist for reducing inequality. Progressive taxes, for example, directly redistribute income. Quality public schools and access to higher education provide an opportunity for people of all income levels to invest in themselves and improve their future incomes. Research on the role of the existing policy mechanisms, as well as identification of new policy options, is essential for understanding how California state policy influences the distribution of income.

Some Americans believe that differences in income arise primarily from individual choices, preferences, abilities, investments, and productivity, and that income inequality is a product of an economy that values hard work and talent. Other Americans believe that income differences reflect the unequal distribution of economic opportunity in our society, and that the opportunity to succeed is elusive for those who do not belong to privileged groups. The first viewpoint implies that public policy can affect inequality only by redistributing income; the second implies that policy can reduce inequality by promoting opportunity. Research on the determinants of income distribution and the extent to which policy provides or restricts economic opportunity will suggest avenues for improving opportunities for the less-advantaged.

If California seeks to reduce income inequality, the state will benefit from research that identifies policy options that promote equity as well as efficiency in our economy.

Labor Market Explanations for Rising Earnings Inequality

The similar trends in California and the nation suggest that the same forces that explain the widening of the income distribution in the United States account for the growth in income inequality in California. At the national level, the rise in male earnings inequality has been explained by a combination of factors. Economists agree that changes in the supply and demand of labor have favored skilled workers over less-skilled workers. The underlying forces that have led to these labor market trends include technological change, international competition, immigration, and deunionization.[1] However, the effect of each of these forces on the distribution of earnings in California's distinct economy remains to be studied.

---

[1]Cassidy (1995) provides a straightforward summary of these explanations for rising earnings inequality.

Many economists believe that technological change has benefited educated workers who are able to implement new technology and has harmed less-educated workers who may be replaced by mechanized production.[2] The effect of technological innovation on California workers may be more pronounced than in the nation. On one hand, the state has a higher percentage of people with at least some college education (23 percent) than the national average (19 percent). On the other hand, the school dropout rate is 14 percent in California, 3 percentage points above the national average of 11 percent.[3]

There is less agreement on the role of international competition in explaining the rise in income inequality. The cost of a low-skilled workforce is higher in the United States than in other countries, particularly developing countries. Thus, the United States increasingly imports manufactured products and textiles, lowering the labor market demand for low-skilled U.S. workers.[4] International competition may have played a different role in the state because California has more Pacific-region trade than the rest of the nation and because a slightly smaller percentage of the state's workforce is in manufacturing (15 percent compared to the national 16 percent).[5]

Growth in immigration may have contributed to the rise in income inequality. Immigrants can adversely affect the wage distribution by

---

[2]Krueger (1993) finds evidence that supports this theory.

[3]Population statistics based on the 1990 Census as reported in U.S. Bureau of the Census (1994), Table 236.

[4]Borjas, Freeman, and Katz (1992) have found evidence that trade patterns account for a substantial part of the wage losses of high school dropouts.

[5]Workforce statistics for 1993 reported in U.S. Bureau of the Census (1994), Table 655.

raising the number of low-wage workers. Furthermore, by increasing the competition for low-skill employment, immigration can lead to a reduction in the wages offered to natives with low skills.[6] The impact of immigration on California is likely to be greater than in the nation, since California has the largest foreign immigration of any state.

The decline in the power of unions has reduced the bargaining power of labor with the likely effect of lowering the wages of labor relative to that of management.[7] The decline of unions is frequently offered as an explanation for the more rapid growth in earnings inequality in the United States than in other industrialized countries.

The sharp rise in income inequality in California beginning in the late 1980s is probably explained, in part, by the same forces that caused the strong recession of the early 1990s. In addition to cuts in defense spending, suggested causes of the severe recession in the state include a decline in residential building, a fall in commercial aircraft orders, and a reduction in spending relative to income.[8] The effect of each of these factors on the distribution of income remains to be studied.

Demographic Explanations for Rising Family Income Inequality

In addition to the economic and labor market forces that explain the increase in earnings inequality in the nation, trends in marriage and

---

[6]Butcher and Card (1991) and Borjas, Freeman, and Katz (1992) find evidence of an effect of immigration on wage inequality.

[7]Freeman (1993) reports evidence that the decline in unions lowered the wages of blue-collar workers relative to wages of white-collar workers.

[8]These factors are discussed in a study by the Center for the Continuing Study of the California Economy (1994).

female labor force participation may contribute to the rise in household and family income inequality.

Declines in the percentage of people who are married may explain a portion of the rise in family income inequality. The growing share of families that rely on the earnings of single mothers has increased the number of low-income families.[9] In addition, low-income men are less likely to be married than high-income men and are thus less likely to have a spouse who contributes to family income.[10] Trends in marriage behavior may have a larger effect in California than in the nation. Compared to the national average, California had a lower rate of marriage and a higher rate of divorce between 1980 and 1992.[11]

The growth in the female labor force participation has an undetermined effect on the distribution of family income. As the percentage of women with earnings increased, earnings inequality among women fell. In addition, the rising earnings of married women have increased family income and reduced inequality among married-couple families.[12] At the same time, however, the increased contribution of the earnings of wives has further polarized the incomes of single people relative to those of married couples. Furthermore, the correlation of the earnings of husbands and wives has increased: The wives of men with high earnings tend to earn more than the wives of men with low

---

[9]Danziger and Gottschalk (1995) find that the rise in female headship increased the poverty rate by 1.6 percentage points between 1973 and 1991 (Table 5.3, p. 102).

[10]Burtless (1996) makes this observation.

[11]Marriage statistics reported in U.S. Bureau of the Census (1994), Table 146.

[12]Cancian, Danziger, and Gottschalk (1993) find that changes in the earnings of married women reduced income inequality among married-couple families between 1968 and 1988.

earnings.[13] The effect of female labor force participation may have been different in California because the increase in the average hours worked by women has been smaller than in the nation.[14]

Additional Measurement Issues

There are a number of measurement issues we could not explore with Census Bureau income data that are important for a more complete understanding of the recent trends in income inequality and their implications for public policy in California. The income data used in this study do not account for the effect of taxes and non-monetary compensation (e.g., housing subsidies, health insurance). While national studies show that using more comprehensive measures of income does not substantially change income inequality trends,[15] the effect may be different in California. For example, the percentage of people in California without health insurance was 19.3 in 1992, compared to a national average of 14.7 percent.[16]

The statistics reported in this study describe the distribution of income in each year. Because a person is likely to occupy different places in the distribution of income during his or her lifetime, the distribution

---

[13]Karoly and Burtless (1995) show the rising correlation of earnings between husbands and wives.

[14]Mean annual hours worked increased from 362 to 576 (59 percent) in California and from 348 to 597 (72 percent) in the United States between 1975 and 1994. These statistics include women who do not work in the labor market (zero hours). Statistics are based on the authors' calculations from the March CPS.

[15]See Appendix C for a brief review of the literature on the distribution trends of more comprehensive measures of income.

[16]Health insurance statistics are reported in U.S. Bureau of the Census (1994), Table 165.

of annual income may not accurately reflect the level of inequality in lifetime income. Research at the national level suggests that economic mobility, the changing of positions within the distribution, has remained stable or declined in recent decades.[17] However, income variability, the year-to-year fluctuations in income, appears to explain a substantial portion of the increase in male earnings inequality.[18] Income mobility and variability remain to be studied in California.

The Challenge for the State

The combination of the sharp rise in household income inequality in California that began even before the most recent recession, the stagnation and decline of male wages, and the decline of household income for the lower and lower-middle ranks of the distribution pose a challenge to public policy in California. Can state policy help to meet the needs of low-income residents of the state and promote economic equity while not sacrificing economic growth? The answer to this question depends on the causes of recent trends and the policy options for the state. Future reports in this series will address these issues.

---

[17]Hungerford (1993) estimates income mobility in the United States in the 1970s and 1980s.

[18]Gottschalk and Moffitt (1994) find that one-third to one-half of the increase in the variance of earnings among white males from the 1970s to the 1980s can be explained by increased earnings instability.

Appendix A

Notes on Data and Methodology

This appendix addresses several limitations of the income data and the adjustments for price inflation and cost of living. When applicable, we describe our methodology for reducing the effect of these limitations on the estimated trends in income inequality.

Income Data

Income data for this study come from two national household surveys collected by the U.S. Bureau of the Census: the decennial Census of Population and Housing (1970, 1980, and 1990)[1] and the

---

[1]1970 Public Use Sample, 1 percent; 1980 and 1990 Public Use Micro Sample, 5 percent.

March Annual Demographic File of the Current Population Survey (public-use files, survey years 1968–1995).[2]

The Current Population Survey (CPS) and the Census report pre-tax, money income, which includes wages, salary, farm income, self-employment income, Social Security, railroad retirement, Supplemental Social Security, public assistance, welfare, interest, dividends, income from estates and trusts, net rental income, veterans' payments, unemployment and workers' compensation, private and government pensions, alimony, child support, regular contributions from persons not living in the same household, and other periodic income. Capital gains are not included.

Current Population Survey

The March file of the CPS, an annual survey of civilian households, provides detailed demographic information, including income received, for about 5,000 households in California and 50,000 households in the nation.[3] The main benefit of using the CPS to study income

---

[2]Each survey has income information from the previous year. This study covers income years 1967–1994. Uniform series data files for CPS survey years 1964–1967, created under the direction of Robert Mare and Christopher Winship, are available from the University of Wisconsin. We chose not to use these files because of possible compatibility problems with the public-use files. We found much smaller average household sizes in the Mare-Winship files relative to the public-use files (e.g., the Mare-Winship file for 1967 had an average household size of 2.4 persons and the public-use file for 1968 had an average household size of 3.2 persons). The increase in household size leads to a sizable drop in adjusted household income between 1966 and 1967, whereas unadjusted household income shows a slight increase. We interpret the change in household size as evidence of a problem with the data and therefore we report statistics beginning with the 1968 public-use files.

[3]The March file of the CPS also includes Armed Forces personnel living with civilians. Our measures of household and family income include these households and families. Samples of workers do not include military personnel. About 3,000–4,000 male workers and 2,000–3,000 female workers are in the California sample. The national samples have about ten times as many workers as the California samples.

distribution is that it contains annual data, making it possible to observe
short-term departures from long-term trends. As this study shows, the
business cycle fluctuations observable in those data have strong effects on
the distribution of income. The CPS allows us to use comparison years
at the same stages of the business cycle when examining inequality
changes over time.

Over the period of the study, several changes were made in the
design of the CPS, which could affect the comparability of the surveys
across years. Survey changes that affect the distribution of income will
result in one-time jumps in the measures of inequality but not in a
pattern of changes across several years. We have confidence in the
measured distribution trends discussed in the text because none of these
results relies on a change that occurred in a single year.

Each decade, the Census Bureau changes the sample design of the
survey using population estimates from the most recent Census. The
Census Bureau randomly selects a new sample of geographic areas called
Primary Sampling Units (PSUs); in California, the PSUs are generally
counties. To make the sample representative of all parts of the state, the
PSUs are selected from groups of counties with similar population
characteristics. Thus, even when the PSUs change, estimates of the
income distribution should not be affected because each new PSU should
be similar to the one it replaced. All significant sample design changes
for this study occurred in 1972–1973 and 1985–1986 (the 1995–1996
redesign was implemented after the March 1995 survey).[4]

---

[4]The Census Bureau does rotate "Enumeration Districts" within the Primary
Sampling Units. However, substitutions in Enumeration Districts are chosen based on

The Census Bureau constructs sample weights such that the CPS sample will represent the national population. The sample weights are based on information from the decennial Census. In survey years 1973, 1982, and 1994, the Census Bureau revised the sample weights to reflect new population estimates from the 1970, 1980, and 1990 Census. Karoly (1993) compares income inequality in the original release of the 1980 CPS and in a reissue of the same survey using the new sample weights. She finds that the change in sampling weights had little effect on the increase in inequality between income years 1978 and 1979.

The Census Bureau has changed the survey procedure with respect to Hispanics. In 1976, an additional sample of 2,000 Hispanic households was added to the March CPS to increase Hispanic representation. These households were chosen randomly from Hispanic households interviewed in the November CPS. The addition of these households could affect the measured distribution of income between income years 1974 and 1975. In 1984, the sample weighting procedure was changed to incorporate Hispanics explicitly. This change increased the estimated number of Hispanics and may have affected the distribution of income.

In 1994, the Census Bureau automated the CPS survey questionnaire and introduced new sample weights. The Census Bureau (1996) reported that these changes may have increased measured income inequality.

Finally, one specific problem with the CPS occurred in a single year of the survey. The median reported income received in 1988 shows an

---

similarity of population characteristics and geographic proximity and should not affect population and income statistics.

anomalous decrease in California. Karoly (1995) also reports a decline in income in California in 1988 based on the CPS data. Measures of income in California from other sources do not suggest a dip in 1988. For example, Department of Commerce data show the level of per capita income in 1988 about midway between 1987 and 1989 (*California Statistical Abstract*, 1995, Table D-7). The probable cause of this reported aberration lies not in California but in Washington. In 1989, funding for the CPS was cut and the sample for California fell to fewer than 3,000 households. The smaller sample size led to a higher sampling error for the 1988 data than in other years and may have affected the representativeness of the sample in that year.[5] For this reason, we do not rely heavily on our results for 1988 in the California data. Funding was restored the following year and the California sample size returned to almost 5,000 in 1990.

Census of Population and Housing

We use the Public Use Sample of the Census to investigate the distribution of income and earnings in 1969, 1979, and 1989. One advantage of using the Census is that its larger sample size leads to more precise statistical estimates. In addition, the Census is designed to survey the entire population and therefore is representative of each state (with the important exception of undercount problems). The main limitation of the Census is that with only three years of data, we cannot distinguish long-run trends from short-run business cycle effects. However, because

---

[5]The sample weights were adjusted to reflect the smaller sample size, but the representativeness of the sample may still have been affected because the sample was not cut randomly, but only in Los Angeles.

the Census years are all business cycle peaks, changes in the distribution of income as reported in the Census are likely to represent trends rather than cyclical fluctuations.

Although we expect to observe similar trends in the distribution of income using the CPS and the Census, income data from the two sources are not identical. For example, in 1990, the Census asked respondents about eight specific types of income. In the same year, the CPS asked about more than 20 types of income, making it less likely that a respondent will omit a source of income than when answering the Census questions. Also, the CPS is collected over the phone by trained survey-takers, who help improve the survey accuracy relative to the Census, which is done by mail. For this reason, we expect the CPS to reflect more accurately the sum of income from all sources as well as earnings and wages.

The changes in the Census survey procedures were not as significant as changes in the CPS for measuring the trends in the distribution of income. It is worth noting that the Public Use Sample in 1970 (1 percent of the population) was much smaller than the Public Use Microdata Samples in 1980 and 1990 (5 percent of the population). Also, income in 1970 was reported as a range (e.g., \$100–\$199); we used the median of the ranges in our calculations. We did not calculate hourly wages with the Census data because the 1970 Census asks about hours of work in the previous week, as opposed to in a usual week in the previous year,[6] and these hours are reported as a range (e.g., 1 to 14 hours).

---

[6]For this same reason, we do not calculate hourly wages in the CPS before 1975.

Top-Codes

Both the CPS and the decennial Census restrict responses to income questions to a certain range. Responses outside of the range are "top-coded": reported at the range cutoff points. For instance, from 1967 to 1975, sampled households with income above $50,000 were reported as income at $50,000 in the CPS. The range for reporting incomes changed over time.

Increasing the magnitude of the top-code can increase measured income inequality even when the true underlying distribution of income does not change. To limit biases in our measures of inequality due to changing top-codes, we standardized the percentage top-coded across every year for each type of income for both surveys. Similarly, we recoded the same percentage in California and the United States. For example, the highest percentage of persons affected by the top-code of household income in the CPS was 98.8 percent (in 1975 in California). We recoded household income in every year of the CPS so that 98.8 percent of people were top-coded in both the state and the nation.

Despite this recode, the top-coding can still affect estimates of trends in income distribution. The recode consistently top-codes total household income but not its component parts. In some cases, a person will have one component of income top-coded so that the sum of household income is affected by this top-code even when his or her household income is below the top of the range for household income. For example, a person with a salary of over $50,000 in 1980 will have that component of his income top-coded. This top-coding will affect the sum of income in his household, even though household income was not top-coded in that year. The measure of annual earnings used in the text is not affected by this problem because we only need to recode based on a single component: income from wages and salary.

The household size adjustment results in an additional problem with top-coding. A household with income top-coded at $50,000 in 1970 may not be in the top of the distribution of adjusted household income in that year if several people share that income.

Top-coding will also dampen the magnitude of levels of inequality by masking the distribution of income above the cutoff points. As a result, an increasing concentration of income among the super-rich (the top 1 percent of income recipients) will not register in our measures of income inequality. Similarly, if the spread of income above the top-code is greater in some areas of the country than in others, the top-code will affect our comparisons of California to other states and regions.

Thus, although we have recoded the data for consistent top-codes, the trends in adjusted household income are still affected by top-coding. Top-coding changed in each Census and in the CPS in years 1976, 1981, 1982, 1985, and 1989.

Imputation Procedures

In both the CPS and the Census, some respondents do not answer some of the income questions or answer inconsistently. When this happens, the Census Bureau uses a "hot deck" procedure to impute the missing income information from another person or household with similar characteristics. The hot deck procedure has changed over time in the CPS and in every year of the Census.

In the CPS in 1976, education was added to the list of items used to define a hot deck match and the procedure was changed so that earnings, weeks of work, and hours per week are supplied by the same matched observation. Juhn, Murphy, and Pierce (1993) show that these changes lowered estimates of hourly wage inequality. The trends in the distribution of hourly wages in this study begin with the 1976 survey and therefore are not affected by this change.

In 1989, the CPS hot deck procedure was changed so that all income items are supplied by the same matched observation. In addition, the processing system was updated and more sources of income were added to the questionnaire. These changes led to an increase in aggregate income. To allow for comparisons with earlier survey years, the 1988 survey was reissued using the new 1989 processing system. Although we report income statistics for income year 1987 only from the reissue of the March 1988 CPS, all statistics in this study were also calculated with the original 1988 survey. A comparison of the results based on the two surveys shows that the new processing system reduces income inequality for all income metrics and all inequality measures, but the change is small. For example, the coefficient of variation of adjusted household income based on the original 1988 survey was 110.9; it was 110.7 based on the reissue with the new processing system. (See Appendix D for the decile levels of income in both issues of the 1988 survey. The original survey is labeled 1987a; the reissue, which we used, is labeled 1987.)

Consumer Price Index and Cost of Living Adjustment

All income statistics reported in this study have been adjusted to 1994 dollars based on the consumer price index computed by the Bureau of Labor Statistics (BLS). The consumer price index for California is calculated by the California Department of Finance based on the population-weighted sum of the consumer price indices for San Francisco and Los Angeles (and San Diego between 1965 and 1986).

The consumer price index used in this report is based on all urban consumers (CPI-U). In 1983, the method for calculating the CPI-U was changed to include a rental equivalence measure for owner-occupied housing. At the national level, the consumer price index was reissued for the years 1967 to 1982 to reflect this change (CPI-U-X1). The CPI-U-X1 series is the preferred price index because the CPI-U overstated inflation during the 1970s due to housing cost estimation procedures; after 1982, the CPI-U is the same as the CPI-U-X1. Because the CPI-U-X1 series is not available at the level of metropolitan areas before 1983, however, the California price index is based on the CPI-U. To construct a CPI-U-X1 series for California, we assumed that the ratio of (CPI-U)/(CPI-U-X1) in the national statistics is the same for the California statistics. Using this assumption and the CPI-U and CPI-U-X1 series for the nation and the CPI-U series for California, we computed an estimate of the CPI-U-X1 for California.

The consumer price index provided by the BLS does not adjust for cost of living differences among regions. If the cost of living is higher in California than the national average, a higher income in California will have less purchasing power than a lower income elsewhere in the nation. Because of the difficulty in measuring the regional cost of living, the BLS stopped reporting this statistic in 1981. It is possible to create a cost of living series using the 1981 estimate of a 8.4 percent[7] higher cost of

---

[7]The BLS reported a cost of living index for 24 standard metropolitan statistical areas (SMSAs) in 1981. Using the BLS index, McMahon (1991) calculated an index of

living in California and adjusting by the California consumer price index to create a yearly cost of living estimate. However, this estimate may not be accurate enough to allow reliable income comparisons between California and the nation. Median household income, reported in Figure 2.1, has been adjusted in this manner. All other statistics and figures reported in the text are insensitive to the cost of living adjustments.

The price and cost of living adjustments for conversion to 1994 California dollars are summarized in Table A.1. The first column shows the CPI-U for California as reported by the California Department of Finance. The second column shows the CPI-U and the fourth column shows the CPI-U-X1 for the nation, as calculated by the BLS. The third column shows our calculation of a CPI-U-X1 for California using the assumptions described above. The fifth column converts Column 3 so that the 1994 value is equal to 1. The sixth column converts Column 4 to reflect the higher cost of living in California. As described above, the series was calculated by making the cost of living 8.41 percent higher in California than in the nation in 1981. To convert income data to 1994 California dollars, we multiply California data by Column 5 and national data by Column 6.

The "Ideal" Data

Several improvements in the quality of the data and the accuracy of the analysis could be made if California were to collect state-level data for

---

108.41 in California (where the population-weighted average for the United States is 100).

Table A.1

Price and Cost of Living Adjustments, California and United States, 1967–1994

Year	1	2	3	4	5	6
	CPI-U		CPI-U-X1		COLA	
	CA	U.S.	CA	U.S.	CA	U.S.
1967	33.0	33.4	35.9	36.3	4.22	4.50
1968	34.4	34.8	37.3	37.7	4.07	4.33
1969	36.1	36.7	38.8	39.4	3.91	4.15
1970	37.9	38.8	40.3	41.3	3.76	3.96
1971	39.3	40.5	41.8	43.1	3.62	3.79
1972	40.6	41.8	43.1	44.4	3.51	3.68
1973	43.0	44.4	45.7	47.2	3.31	3.46
1974	47.4	49.3	49.9	51.9	3.04	3.15
1975	52.3	53.8	54.6	56.2	2.77	2.91
1976	55.6	56.9	58.0	59.4	2.61	2.75
1977	59.5	60.6	62.1	63.2	2.44	2.58
1978	64.4	65.2	66.7	67.5	2.27	2.42
1979	71.3	72.6	72.7	74.0	2.08	2.21
1980	82.4	82.4	82.3	82.3	1.84	1.98
1981	91.4	90.9	90.6	90.1	1.67	1.81
1982	97.3	96.5	96.4	95.6	1.57	1.71
1983	98.9	99.6	98.9	99.6	1.53	1.64
1984	103.8	103.9	103.8	103.9	1.46	1.57
1985	108.6	107.6	108.6	107.6	1.40	1.52
1986	112.0	109.6	112.0	109.6	1.35	1.49
1987	116.6	113.6	116.6	113.6	1.30	1.44
1988	121.9	118.3	121.9	118.3	1.24	1.38
1989	128.0	124.0	128.0	124.0	1.18	1.32
1990	135.0	130.7	135.0	130.7	1.12	1.25
1991	140.6	136.2	140.6	136.2	1.08	1.20
1992	145.6	140.3	145.6	140.3	1.04	1.16
1993	149.4	144.5	149.4	144.5	1.01	1.13
1994	151.5	148.2	151.5	148.2	1.00	1.10

SOURCES: Column 1, California Department of Finance; Columns 2 and 4, U.S. Bureau of Labor Statistics; Columns 3, 5, and 6, authors' calculations.

the study of the economy, including income inequality. Ideally, the state dataset would use a sample representative of the population of California that would be big enough to look at subregions and groups within the population. The dataset would be consistently collected over several years and would include a panel component (i.e., would interview the same people over time). It would add to the value of the survey to have accurate inflation and cost of living estimates for the state.

Appendix B

Using the Current Population Survey to Represent California[1]

The weighting procedure in the Current Population Survey (CPS) makes the survey representative of the nation as a whole. In calculating the March file weights, the Census Bureau does not attempt to correct for population distributions within states (e.g., California's distinct racial distribution). Therefore, the California subsample of the March CPS may not accurately represent the population of the state. Before beginning our analysis of the distribution of income in California based

---

[1]The information on Census Bureau weighting procedures comes from the U.S. Department of Commerce and the Bureau of the Census (1978) and subsequent publications regarding redesign and revision of the CPS.

on the CPS data, we first evaluated the ability of the CPS to represent California.[2]

After conducting the March survey, the Census Bureau calculates a weight for each observation in the sample. The weight is based on a combination of factors, including adjustments to make the survey population match the national population's distributions of age, sex, and race (with full interactions: age within sex within race). In survey years before 1978, the national sample weights did not specifically take into account the total number of people within each state. Since that time, several changes have been implemented in the calculation of the weights so that estimates of state populations based on the CPS sample are consistent with estimates of state total populations from other sources. However, the estimates of state populations within sex, age, and racial groups are not adjusted by the state-specific weights.

Compared to the nation, California has had very different distributions of these characteristics, especially race. We suspected that adjusting the sample to match the U.S. distributions might severely affect the sample distributions for California. Furthermore, the Census Bureau bases the national weights on the decennial Census. Between Census updates, the weights are based on calculations of the population change. California's distinct population trends provide another reason to suspect that the sample distributions would not accurately reflect the changes in California's population.

---

[2]In addition to weighting procedures, sample design issues (e.g., changes in Primary Sampling Units) can also affect the representativeness of the CPS at the state level. The CPS sample design is discussed in Appendix A.

The Census Bureau does calculate labor force estimates at the state level from the CPS. For some states, this requires a state supplemental sample. However, the Census Bureau deemed the California subsample in the CPS large enough to make a state supplement for California unnecessary. Thus, we anticipated that the potential problem for our study was not sample size but rather whether the population distributions would be representative of the state.

Although the Census Bureau believes that the California sample is large enough, it does construct state-specific weights (based on each state's population distribution of race by residence) when it calculates state-specific labor force statistics from the CPS. The Census Bureau's state-specific sample weights are not calculated for the March demographic survey used in this study (and are not provided in the public-use data). However, if the California subsample is found to be not representative of the state, state-specific weights for California could be constructed for the March survey using estimates of the California population by age, sex, and race (available from the Department of Finance).

To determine whether a reweight of the California data was necessary, we evaluated the California subsample of the CPS on the distributions of residence, sex, age, and race—the same characteristics that the Census Bureau uses to weight the national sample. The CPS distributions were compared to the Census distributions for the years 1970, 1980, and 1990.[3] Although the Census is also a national survey, it

____

[3] We expected that the representativeness of the CPS would be particularly poor in Census years. The Census Bureau recalculates the national weights based on each Census and applies updates of them in subsequent years—new weights were introduced in 1973, 1982, and 1994. Therefore, the weights in Census years are based on updates of ten-year-old population estimates.

is designed to survey the entire population in each state. The 5 percent sample of the Census used in this study is randomly chosen from the national population and is therefore representative at the state level (except for undercount problems).

Table B.1 reports the distributions of farm households, sex, age, race, and ethnicity for California from the Census and the CPS.[4] Judging by the similarity of the distributions, we concluded that the California subsample of the national CPS appears to represent the California population accurately with respect to these characteristics. Thus, we used the national sample weights in our calculations and did not reweight at the California level.

The race and ethnicity distributions do show an interesting difference between the CPS and the Census. In 1980 and 1990, the distributions of race in the CPS do not match well with the distributions of race in the Census. However, when race and ethnicity are combined, the distributions from the two surveys match closely. This pattern suggests that people respond differently to race questions in the CPS and in the Census. Hispanic respondents in the Census are much more likely to record race as "other" than Hispanic respondents in the CPS.

Although the statistics reported in Table B.1 certainly suggest that the California subsample of the CPS can be used to represent the state, further research is required to verify that the interacted distributions (sex within age within race) and the intercensal distributions are representative. Such verification is beyond the scope of this report.

____

[4]Deciles of the income distributions in the CPS and the Census also match fairly closely. See Appendix D.

Table B.1

Percentage of Population in Each Category: Census and CPS

Characteristic	1970 Census	1970 CPS	1980 Census	1980 CPS	1990 Census	1990 CPS
Farm						
% non-farm household	90	n/a	99	99	99	99
Sex						
% male	48	48	49	49	49	49
Age in years						
0–4	8	9	8	8	8	9
5–9	10	11	7	7	8	8
10–14	10	10	8	7	7	7
15–19	9	9	9	9	7	7
20–24	8	8	9	10	8	8
25–29	7	7	9	9	9	9
30–34	6	6	9	9	10	9
35–39	6	6	7	6	8	8
40–44	6	6	5	5	7	7
45–49	6	7	5	5	6	5
50–54	5	5	5	5	5	4
55–59	5	5	5	5	4	4
60–64	4	3	4	4	4	4
65–69	3	3	4	4	4	4
70–74	2	2	3	3	3	3
75–79	2	2	2	2	2	2
80+	2	2	2	2	2	2
Hispanic						
Mexican	n/a	n/a	15	15	21	21
Other Hispanic	n/a	n/a	4	3	5	4
Not Hispanic	n/a	n/a	80	82	74	75
Race						
White	90	90	77	86	69	83
Black	7	6	8	8	7	7
Native American	n/a	n/a	n/a	n/a	1	1
Asian	n/a	n/a	n/a	n/a	10	9
Other	3	4	16	6	13	1
Race and ethnicity						
White, non-Hispanic	n/a	n/a	67	68	57	58
Black, non-Hispanic	n/a	n/a	7	8	7	7
Asian, non-Hispanic	n/a	n/a	5	n/a	9	9
Hispanic	n/a	n/a	19	18	26	25
Other, non-Hispanic	n/a	n/a	1	6	1	1

SOURCES: Authors' calculations from the March CPS and the Census.

NOTE: Percentages may not add to 100 due to rounding.

86

Appendix C

Trends in the Distributions of Alternative Measures of Income

The first section of this appendix reviews the literature on the trends in the distributions of income for measures that account for taxes and non-monetary compensation and transfers. The second section presents results for alternative measures of money income not discussed fully in the text.

Income Other Than Money Income

The Current Population Survey (CPS) and the Census measure only pre-tax money income. When taxes and non-monetary transfers (e.g., health insurance, housing subsidies) are incorporated in the income measure, the decline in annual earnings is often diminished and the level of income inequality is generally lower. However, national research shows that the growth in income inequality remains at levels similar to pre-tax money income.

Pre-tax money income measures are imperfect indices of economic well-being. Money income is not reduced for payments such as personal taxes, Social Security, and union dues. Money income does not include non-monetary compensation such as health insurance, employer contributions to retirement programs, and room and board. Money income also does not include non-monetary transfers such as Medi-Cal, housing subsidies, food stamps, and energy assistance. Money income does not include the return to non-financial investments, such as owner-occupied housing.

Studies that adjust money income for tax payments have reported rising inequality trends similar to those found for pre-tax income. Chamberlain and Spillberg (1991) report that the share of pre-tax adjusted gross income going to the top 20 percent of the distribution increased 9.5 percent between 1980 and 1988; the share of after-tax income increased 9.3 percent. Moreover, Gramlich, Kasten, and Sammartino (1993) and Pechman (1990) find that for the nation during the 1980s, inequality in after-tax income increased even more than inequality in pre-tax income.

National studies that attempt to account for non-monetary benefits and taxes find that the trends in money income inequality are confirmed. The U.S. House of Representatives Committee on Ways and Means (1989) reports similar trends in the quintile shares of money income and more comprehensive income (after-tax income, including food and housing benefits). For example, the share of money income received by the poorest 20 percent of families fell by 9.8 percent between 1979 and

1987; their share of comprehensive income fell by 9.2 percent. Levy (1987) finds that the level of income inequality is lower when taxes, Medicare, Medicaid, food stamps, and fringe benefits are included in income, but that the trends in income inequality in Census and CPS data are essentially the same. This result may be different in California, which has lower health insurance rates than the rest of the country.

Consumption data provide an alternative measure of economic well-being. Cutler and Katz (1991, 1992) find that changes in the distribution of expenditures parallel changes in the distribution of money income during the 1980s.

Alternative Measures of Money Income

Chapter 2 describes trends in the distribution of adjusted household income among persons. This measure of income was chosen because it allows for income-sharing among members of the same household, accounts for the greater income needs of large households, and counts each person equally regardless of household size. With CPS data it is possible to create alternative measures of income that vary the income-pooling unit (e.g., income-sharing within the family versus within the household), the size adjustment, and the unit of analysis (e.g., each person counts as a unit versus each household counts as a unit). Table C.1 lists the 12 types of household and family income examined in this study. All 12 measures use the sum of income received from all reported sources.

Chapter 3 describes the trends in the distributions of annual earnings and hourly wages among people who are primarily employees (i.e., people who receive most of their earnings from wages and salary as

Table C.1

Alternative Measures of Household and Family Income

	Income Measure	Income Pooling	Unit of Analysis	Size Adjustment	Location of Results
1.	Adjusted household income among persons	Household residents	Person	$\sqrt{n}$	Chapter 2
2.	Unadjusted household income among persons	Household residents	Person	None	Appendix C
3.	Adjusted household income among households	Household residents	Household	$\sqrt{n}$	Appendix C
4.	Unadjusted household income among households	Household residents	Household	None	Appendix C
5.	Adjusted family income among persons	Family members	Person	$\sqrt{n}$	Chapter 2
6.	Unadjusted family income among persons	Family members	Person	None	Appendix C
7.	Adjusted family income among families	Family members	Family	$\sqrt{n}$	Appendix C
8.	Unadjusted family income among families	Family members	Family	None	Appendix C
9.	Adjusted primary family income among persons	Primary family members	Person	$\sqrt{n}$	Appendix C
10.	Unadjusted primary family income among persons	Primary family members	Person	None	Appendix C
11.	Adjusted primary family income among families	Primary family members	Family	$\sqrt{n}$	Appendix C
12.	Unadjusted primary family income among families	Primary family members	Family	None	Appendix C

NOTES: A "family" includes all people living in the same household who are related by blood, marriage, or adoption. Separate family observations are created for single people and secondary families (families not related to their head of household). A "primary family" includes the head of household and relatives. Single people and secondary families are excluded. There is only one primary family per household.

opposed to farm ownership and self-employment). The sample was restricted to employees because income from self-employment and one's own farm often includes not only income from labor but also income from capital investments. To ensure that the measured trends were not a result of limiting the sample to employees, the study also examined the distributions of annual earnings and hourly wages without this sample restriction. In addition, we examined the distributions limited to workers ages 18 to 55 (to remove any effects of early retirement) and the distributions of income from wages and salary only (for comparison to earlier national studies). Table C.2 summarizes the seven measures of labor income examined in this study. The trends in each income measure were estimated for males and females separately.

The alternative measures generally display similar results to those discussed in the text. For family income and male earnings and hourly wages, we find the same five results: Inequality has increased in California since the early 1970s, the level and trends in inequality were similar in California and the nation until the late 1980s when inequality in California grew more rapidly, inequality increased most rapidly during recessions, income in the lower percentiles declined, and income growth was slower in California than in the nation.

There are few exceptions to these trends. When family income is weighted at the family level, the VLN measure of inequality shows that California had higher inequality as early as 1979. When male annual earnings includes all workers, the VLN measure shows higher inequality in the United States than in California before 1975 and no substantial difference between the United States and California in the 1990s. For male income from wages and salary, the level of the VLN measure of inequality essentially recovers to pre-recession levels after the recession of the early 1980s. Despite these differences, the basic trends remain fairly consistent and the measures of income discussed in the text are preferred (as discussed above).

Table C.2

Alternative Measures of Labor Income

Income Measure	Sample Includes Anyone Who:	Source of Earnings	Unit	Ages	Location of Results
13. Male annual earnings among workers 20. Female annual earnings among workers	Receives earnings primarily from wages and salary	All earnings	Annual	18 and over	Chapter 3
14. Male hourly wages among workers 21 Female hourly wages among workers	Receives earnings primarily from wages and salary	All earnings	Hourly	18 and over	Chapter 3
15. Male annual earnings, workers ages 18 to 55 22. Female annual earnings, workers ages 18 to 55	Receives earnings primarily from wages and salary	All earnings	Annual	18 to 55	Appendix C
16. Male hourly wages, workers ages 18 to 55 23. Female hourly wages, workers ages 18 to 55	Receives earnings primarily from wages and salary	All earnings	Hourly	18 to 55	Appendix C
17. Male annual earnings among all workers 24. Female annual earnings among all workers	Receives income from wages, salary, self-employment, or own farm	All earnings	Annual	18 and over	Appendix C

Table C.2—continued

Income Measure	Sample Includes Anyone Who:	Source of Earnings	Unit	Ages	Location of Results
18. Male hourly wages among all workers	Receives income from wages, salary, self-employment, or own farm	All earnings	Hourly	18 and over	Appendix C
25. Female hourly wages among all workers					
19. Male annual wages and salary	Receives any income from wages and salary	Earnings from wages and salary	Annual	18 and over	Appendix C
26. Female annual wages and salary					

NOTES: The income category "Receives earnings primarily from wages and salary" excludes people who report more income from their farm or business than from wages and salaries and excludes any person reporting an absolute value of more than $2,000 in 1994 dollars in income from their own farm or self-employment. Some wage and salary workers included in the sample receive a small amount of income from farms and self-employment. This income was included in annual earnings to improve estimates of hourly wages because estimates of annual hours of work include hours worked in the farm or business. The income category "All earnings" includes earnings from wages, salary, self-employment, or own farm. Hourly wages are not calculated for income types 19 and 26 because hours of work includes hours worked in self-employment or own farm. All samples exclude military personnel, students, people with earnings less than or equal to zero, people under age 18, and workers whose primary occupation is "without pay."

The trends in the distribution of household income show more sensitivity to the adjustments for household size and weighting by persons. When each household is counted as a single unit (as opposed to each person) or no adjustments are made for household size, the upward trend in the VLN is less clear. Household income growth is generally, but not always, higher in the United States than in California. When household income is weighted at the household level, income at the 20th percentile does not decline between 1969 and 1989, but it does decline between 1976 and 1994. Although these differences are notable, unadjusted and unweighted household income does not reflect economic well-being as accurately as adjusted household income (weighted at the person level) because it does not adjust for the greater needs of large households and it gives less weight to people in large households.

For all the measures of female annual earnings, inequality declined until the early 1980s, the level and trends in inequality were similar in California and the nation, and income in the lower percentiles increased. When female annual earnings are measured for all female workers regardless of self-employment or own farm status, the decline in inequality does not begin until after 1975 and all measures of inequality show a rising trend after 1983. This is in contrast to the trends discussed in the text for female annual earnings among workers who receive earnings primarily from wages and salary: The trends in inequality after the early 1980s depended on which measure of inequality was used.

For the measures of female hourly wages, inequality has increased since the early 1980s, the level and trends in inequality were similar in California and the nation, and wages in the lower percentiles fell. There were no substantial exceptions to this pattern.

For annual earnings and hourly wages among both males and females, the trends in the distributions remain nearly identical when the age range is restricted to ages 18 to 55.

Tables C.3 through C.22 and their associated figures provide summary statistics for the trends in the distributions of each alternative measure of income that is not described fully in the text.

Table C.3

Percentage Change in Real Unadjusted Household Income Among Persons Between Selected Years, by Income Percentile

	Business Cycle Peaks			Recessions
	1969–1979	1979–1989	1969–1989	1976–1994
California				
20th	–7	–2	–8	–20
Median	4	2	7	–2
80th	13	7	21	14
Change in 80/20 ratio (%)	+21	+9	+32	+42
United States				
20th	–1	–1	–2	–7
Median	9	3	12	2
80th	14	11	27	15
Change in 80/20 ratio (%)	+15	+13	+29	+24

SOURCE: Based on authors' calculations from the March CPS.

NOTE: Statistics reported in this table are sensitive to the consumer price index, except for the 80/20 ratio.

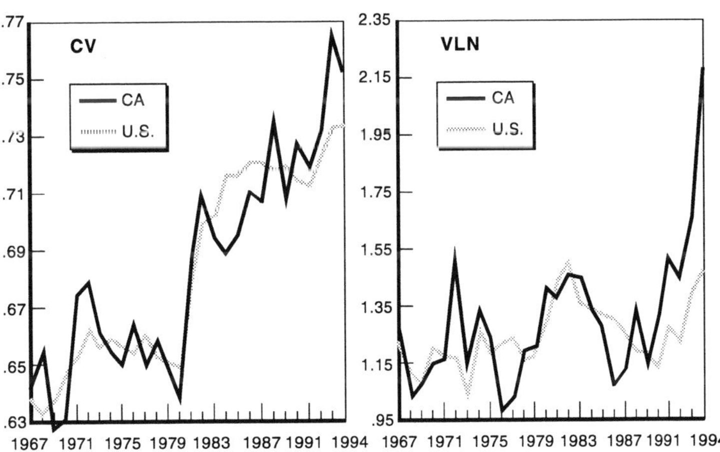

SOURCE: Based on authors' calculations from the March CPS.

NOTE: Statistics reported in this figure are not sensitive to the consumer price index.

Figure C.1—Summary Measures of Inequality for Unadjusted Household Income Among Persons, 1967–1994

Table C.4
Percentage Change in Real Adjusted Household Income Among Households Between Selected Years, by Income Percentile

	Business Cycle Peaks			Recessions
	1969–1979	1979–1989	1969–1989	1976–1994
California				
20th	0	8	8	−11
Median	11	8	19	3
80th	18	10	30	17
Change in 80/20 ratio (%)	+18	+2	+20	+31
United States				
20th	13	5	18	5
Median	15	10	26	9
80th	18	14	36	20
Change in 80/20 ratio (%)	+5	+9	+15	+15

SOURCE: Based on authors' calculations from the March CPS.

NOTE: Statistics reported in this table are sensitive to the consumer price index, except for the 80/20 ratio.

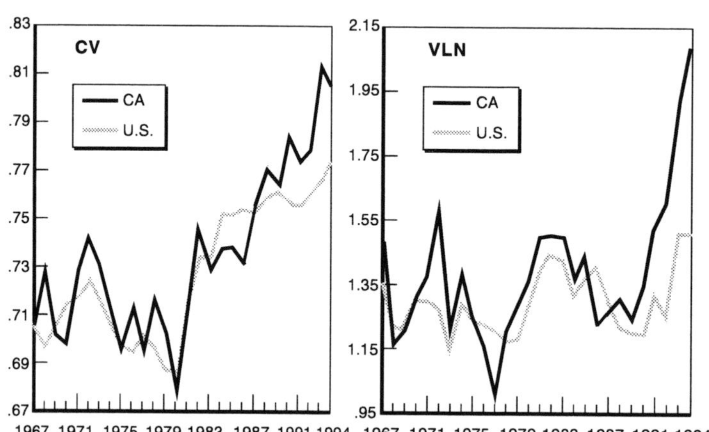

SOURCE: Based on authors' calculations from the March CPS.

NOTE: Statistics reported in this figure are not sensitive to the consumer price index.

Figure C.2—Summary Measures of Inequality for Adjusted Household Income Among Households, 1967–1994

Income Type 4: Unadjusted Household Income, Weighted at the Household Level

Table C.5

Percentage Change in Real Unadjusted Household Income Among Households Between Selected Years, by Income Percentile

	Business Cycle Peaks			Recessions
	1969–1979	1979–1989	1969–1989	1976–1994
California				
20th	–3	14	10	–9
Median	2	6	8	4
80th	10	10	21	18
Change in 80/20 ratio (%)	+13	–3	+10	+29
United States				
20th	3	4	7	0
Median	5	5	11	2
80th	11	11	23	14
Change in 80/20 ratio (%)	+8	+7	+15	+15

SOURCE: Based on authors' calculations from the March CPS.

NOTE: Statistics reported in this table are sensitive to the consumer price index, except for the 80/20 ratio.

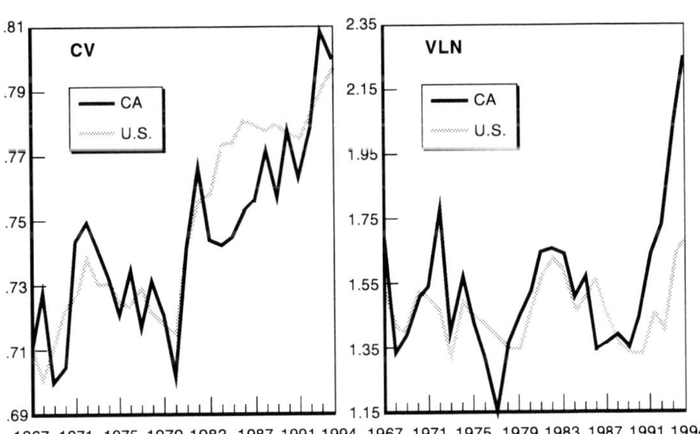

SOURCE: Based on authors' calculations from the March CPS.

NOTE: Statistics reported in this figure are not sensitive to the consumer price index.

Figure C.3—Summary Measures of Inequality for Unadjusted Household Income Among Households, 1967–1994

Table C.6

Percentage Change in Real Unadjusted Family Income Among Persons Between Selected Years, by Income Percentile

	Business Cycle Peaks			Recessions
	1969–1979	1979–1989	1969–1989	1976–1994
California				
20th	–15	–4	–18	–25
Median	1	–2	0	–8
80th	10	6	16	12
Change in 80/20 ratio (%)	+29	+10	+42	+50
United States				
20th	–4	–5	–9	–14
Median	7	1	8	–2
80th	12	10	23	13
Change in 80/20 ratio (%)	+17	+15	+35	+31

SOURCE: Based on authors' calculations from the March CPS.

NOTE: Statistics reported in this table are sensitive to the consumer price index, except for the 80/20 ratio.

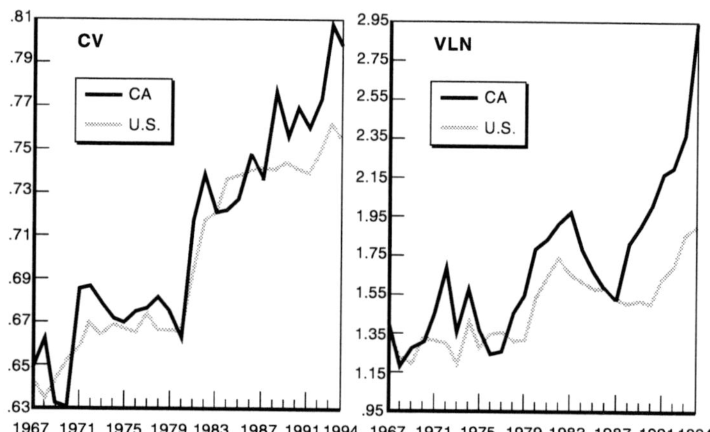

SOURCE: Based on authors' calculations from the March CPS.

NOTE: Statistics reported in this figure are not sensitive to the consumer price index.

Figure C.4—Summary Measures of Inequality for Unadjusted Family Income Among Persons, 1967–1994

Income Type 7: Adjusted Family Income, Weighted at the Family Level

Table C.7

Percentage Change in Real Adjusted Family Income Among
Families Between Selected Years, by Income Percentile

| | Business Cycle Peaks | | | Recessions |
	1969–1979	1979–1989	1969–1989	1976–1994
California				
20th	0	−1	−1	−16
Median	6	6	12	−2
80th	15	7	23	13
Change in 80/20 ratio (%)	+15	+9	+25	+34
United States				
20th	12	2	14	0
Median	13	8	21	6
80th	17	13	33	17
Change in 80/20 ratio (%)	+5	+11	+16	+17

SOURCE: Based on authors' calculations from the March CPS.

NOTE: Statistics reported in this table are sensitive to the consumer price index, except for the 80/20 ratio.

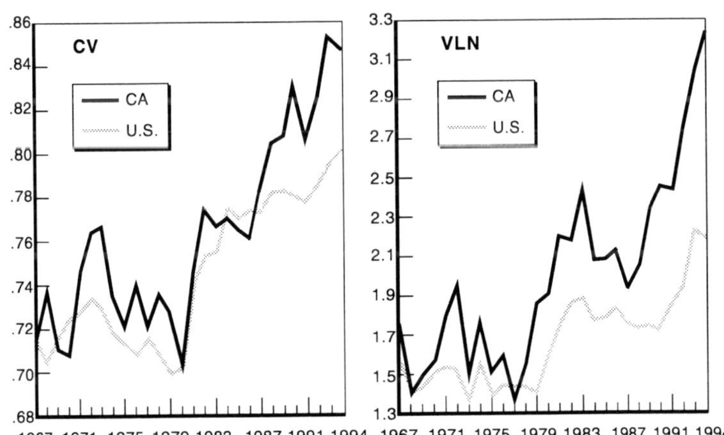

SOURCE: Based on authors' calculations from the March CPS.

NOTE: Statistics reported in this figure are not sensitive to the consumer price index.

Figure C.5—Summary Measures of Inequality for Adjusted
Family Income Among Families, 1967–1994

Income Type 8: Unadjusted Family Income, Weighted at the Family Level

Table C.8

Percentage Change in Real Unadjusted Family Income Among Families Between Selected Years, by Income Percentile

	Business Cycle Peaks			Recessions
	1969–1979	1979–1989	1969–1989	1976–1994
California				
20th	–12	4	–9	–15
Median	–8	3	–5	–5
80th	5	5	11	12
Change in 80/20 ratio (%)	+19	+2	+22	+32
United States				
20th	2	0	2	–8
Median	1	2	3	–5
80th	10	8	19	10
Change in 80/20 ratio (%)	+7	+8	+17	+20

SOURCE: Based on authors' calculations from the March CPS.

NOTE: Statistics reported in this table are sensitive to the consumer price index, except for the 80/20 ratio.

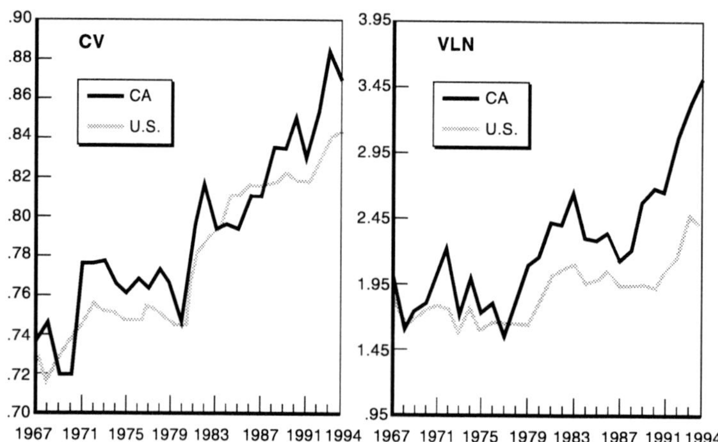

SOURCE: Based on authors' calculations from the March CPS.

NOTE: Statistics reported in this figure are not sensitive to the consumer price index.

Figure C.6—Summary Measures of Inequality for Unadjusted Family Income Among Families, 1967–1994

Income Type 9: Adjusted Primary Family Income, Weighted by Persons

Table C.9

Percentage Change in Real Adjusted Primary Family Income Among
Persons Between Selected Years, by Income Percentile

	Business Cycle Peaks			Recessions
	1969–1979	1979–1989	1969–1989	1976–1994
California				
20th	2	–13	–11	–28
Median	14	0	14	–5
80th	20	5	25	15
Change in 80/20 ratio (%)	+18	+20	+42	+59
United States				
20th	10	–2	9	–4
Median	18	7	27	9
80th	22	13	38	21
Change in 80/20 ratio (%)	+10	+15	+27	+26

SOURCE: Based on authors' calculations from the March CPS.

NOTE: Statistics reported in this table are sensitive to the consumer
price index, except for the 80/20 ratio.

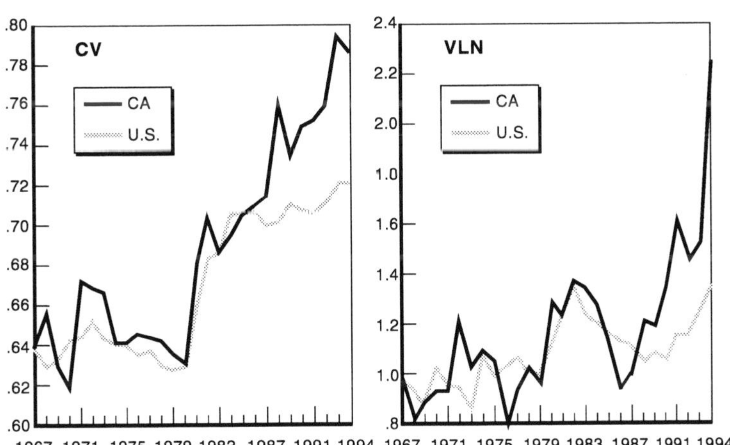

SOURCE: Based on authors' calculations from the March CPS.

NOTE: Statistics reported in this figure are not sensitive to the consumer price index.

Figure C.7—Summary Measures of Inequality for Adjusted
Primary Family Income Among Persons, 1967–1994

Table C.10

Percentage Change in Real Unadjusted Primary Family Income
Among Persons Between Selected Years, by Income Percentile

	Business Cycle Peaks			Recessions
	1969–1979	1979–1989	1969–1989	1976–1994
California				
20th	–15	–4	–18	–25
Median	1	–2	0	–8
80th	10	6	16	12
Change in				
80/20 ratio (%)	+29	+10	+42	+50
United States				
20th	–4	–5	–9	–14
Median	7	1	8	–2
80th	12	10	23	13
Change in				
80/20 ratio (%)	+17	+15	+35	+31

SOURCE: Based on authors' calculations from the March CPS.

NOTE: Statistics reported in this table are sensitive to the consumer price index, except for the 80/20 ratio.

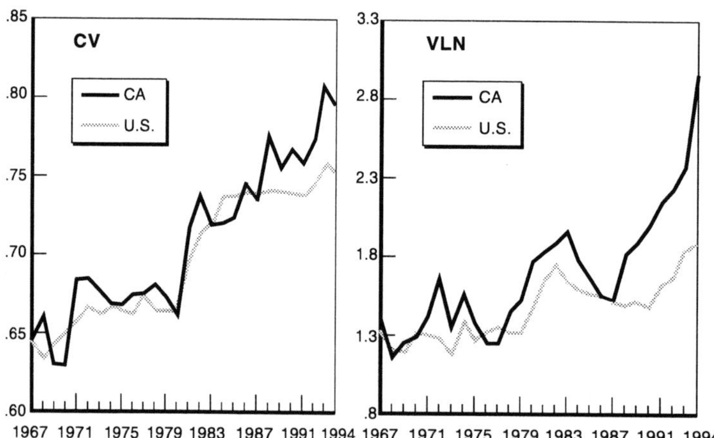

SOURCE: Based on authors' calculations from the March CPS.

NOTE: Statistics reported in this figure are not sensitive to the consumer price index.

**Figure C.8—Summary Measures of Inequality for Unadjusted
Primary Family Income Among Persons, 1967–1994**

Income Type 11: Adjusted Primary Family Income, Weighted at the Family Level

Table C.11

Percentage Change in Real Adjusted Primary Family Income Among Families Between Selected Years, by Income Percentile

	Business Cycle Peaks			Recessions
	1969–1979	1979–1989	1969–1989	1976–1994
California				
20th	1	–8	–8	–23
Median	11	2	14	1
80th	19	6	27	16
Change in 80/20 ratio (%)	+19	+16	+37	+51
United States				
20th	10	–1	10	–1
Median	16	8	25	8
80th	19	15	36	21
Change in 80/20 ratio (%)	+8	+15	+24	+23

SOURCE; Based on authors' calculations from the March CPS.

NOTE: Statistics reported in this table are sensitive to the consumer price index, except for the 80/20 ratio.

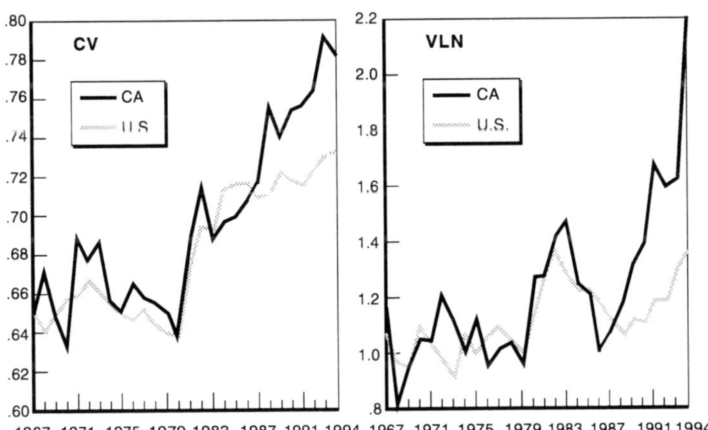

SOURCE: Based on authors' calculations from the March CPS.

NOTE: Statistics reported in this figure are not sensitive to the consumer price index.

Figure C.9—Summary Measures of Inequality for Adjusted Primary Family Income Among Families, 1967–1994

Income Type 12: Unadjusted Primary Family Income, Weighted at the
Family Level

Table C.12

Percentage Change in Real Unadjusted Primary Family Income
Among Families Between Selected Years, by Income Percentile

	Business Cycle Peaks			Recessions
	1969–1979	1979–1989	1969–1989	1976–1994
California				
20th	–3	–5	–8	–20
Median	7	1	9	0
80th	14	8	23	16
Change in 80/20 ratio (%)	+18	+13	+33	+44
United States				
20th	5	–3	2	–4
Median	11	4	16	4
80th	14	13	29	17
Change in 80/20 ratio (%)	+9	+16	+26	+22

SOURCE: Based on authors' calculations from the March CPS.

NOTE: Statistics reported in this table are sensitive to the consumer price index, except for the 80/20 ratio.

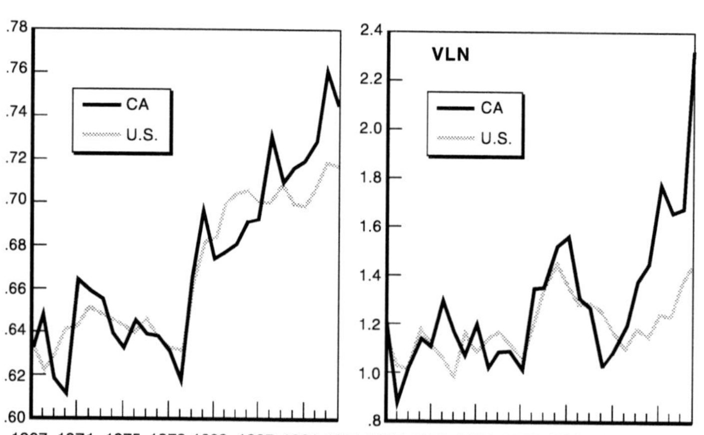

SOURCE: Based on authors' calculations from the March CPS.

NOTE: Statistics reported in this figure are not sensitive to the consumer price index.

Figure C.10—Summary Measures of Inequality for Unadjusted
Primary Family Income Among Families, 1967–1994

Income Type 15: Annual Earnings Among Male Workers Ages 18 to 55

Table C.13

Percentage Change in Real Annual Earnings for Males Ages 18 to 55 Between Selected Years, by Income Percentile

	Business Cycle Peaks			Recessions
	1969–1979	1979–1989	1969–1989	1976–1994
California				
20th	–22	–22	–39	–30
Median	–6	–12	–17	–23
80th	10	–5	4	2
Change in 80/20 ratio (%)	+40	+22	+71	+46
United States				
20th	–7	–17	–22	–20
Median	3	–8	–5	–13
80th	11	4	16	2
Change in 80/20 ratio (%)	+19	+25	+49	+27

SOURCE: Based on authors' calculations from the March CPS.

NOTE: Statistics reported in this table are sensitive to the consumer price index, except for the 80/20 ratio.

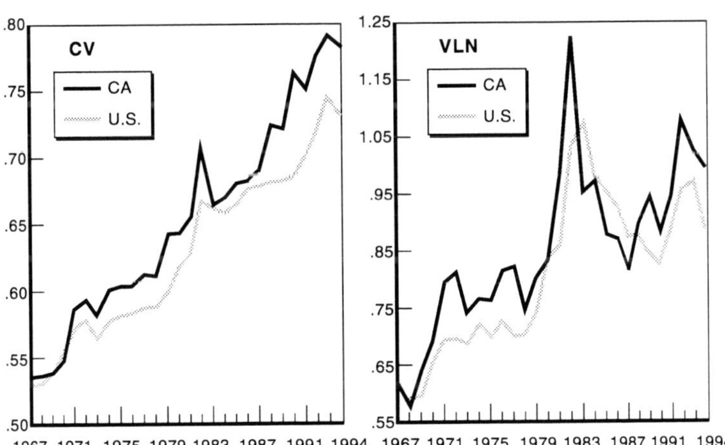

SOURCE: Based on authors' calculations from the March CPS.

NOTE: Statistics reported in this figure are not sensitive to the consumer price index.

Figure C.11—Summary Measures of Inequality for Annual Earnings for Males Ages 18 to 55, 1967–1994

Income Type 16: Hourly Wages Among Male Workers Ages 18 to 55

Table C.14

Percentage Change in Real Hourly Wages for Males Ages 18 to 55 Between Selected Years, by Income Percentile

	Business Cycle Peaks	Recessions
	1979–1989	1976–1994
California		
20th	–21	–31
Median	–14	–23
80th	–5	–6
Change in 80/20 ratio (%)	+20	+36
United States		
20th	–13	–20
Median	–8	–13
80th	1	–2
Change in 80/20 ratio (%)	+16	+22

SOURCE: Based on authors' calculations from the March CPS.

NOTE: Statistics reported in this table are sensitive to the consumer price index, except for the 80/20 ratio.

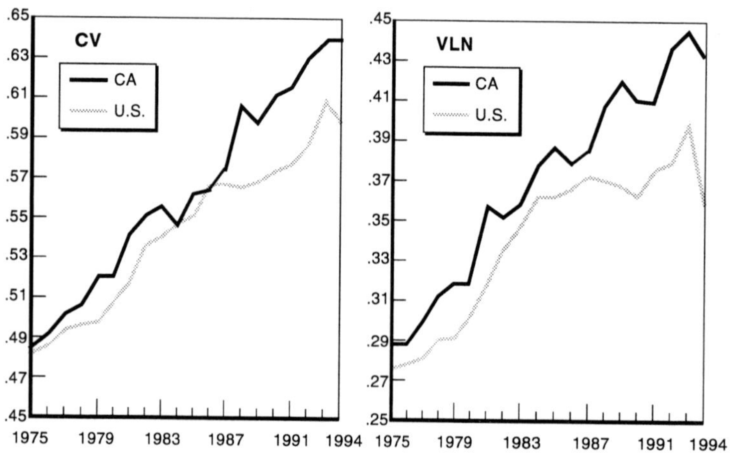

SOURCE: Based on authors' calculations from the March CPS.

NOTE: Statistics reported in this figure are not sensitive to the consumer price index.

Figure C.12—Summary Measures of Inequality for Hourly Wages for Males Ages 18 to 55, 1975–1994

Income Type 17: Annual Earnings Among All Male Workers

Table C.15

Percentage Change in Real Annual Earnings for All Male Workers Between Selected Years, by Income Percentile

	Business Cycle Peaks			Recessions
	1969–1979	1979–1989	1969–1989	1976–1994
California				
20th	–13	–19	–30	–31
median	–5	–10	–14	–20
80th	6	–2	4	–2
Change in 80/20 ratio (%)	+22	+20	+47	+41
United States				
20th	–5	–14	–18	–15
median	3	–5	–2	–12
80th	10	4	15	3
Change in 80/20 ratio (%)	+15	+21	+40	+21

SOURCE: Based on authors' calculations from the March CPS.

NOTE: Statistics reported in this table are sensitive to the consumer price index, except for the 80/20 ratio.

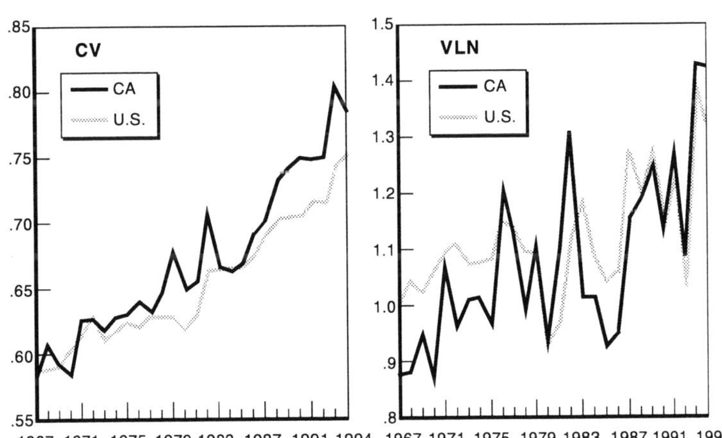

SOURCE: Based on authors' calculations from the March CPS.

NOTE: Statistics reported in this figure are not sensitive to the consumer price index.

Figure C.13—Summary Measures of Inequality for Annual Earnings for All Male Workers, 1967–1994

Income Type 18: Hourly Wages Among All Male Workers

Table C.16

Percentage Change in Real Hourly Wages for All Male
Workers Between Selected Years, by Income Percentile

	Business Cycle Peaks	Recessions
	1979–1989	1976–1994
California		
20th	–19	–30
Median	–12	–21
80th	–4	–4
Change in 80/20 ratio (%)	+19	+37
United States		
20th	–10	–16
Median	–5	–13
80th	2	0
Change in 80/20 ratio (%)	+13	+20

SOURCE: Based on authors' calculations from the March CPS.

NOTE: Statistics reported in this table are sensitive to the consumer price index, except for the 80/20 ratio.

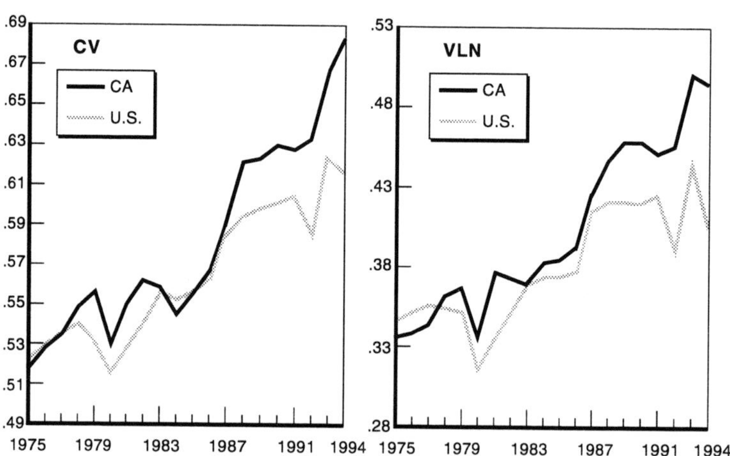

SOURCE: Based on authors' calculations from the March CPS.

NOTE: Statistics reported in this figure are not sensitive to the consumer price index.

Figure C.14—Summary Measures of Inequality for Hourly
Wages for All Male Workers, 1975–1994

Table C.17

Percentage Change in Real Annual Salary for Males
Between Selected Years, by Income Percentile

	Business Cycle Peaks			Recessions
	1969–1979	1979–1989	1969–1989	1976–1994
California				
20th	–3	–14	–16	–14
Median	–4	–12	–15	–23
80th	6	–1	6	4
Change in 80/20 ratio (%)	+9	+15	+26	+21
United States				
20th	–5	–5	–10	–3
Median	5	–6	–1	–8
80th	8	6	15	6
Change in 80/20 ratio (%)	+14	+12	+28	+10

SOURCE: Based on authors' calculations from the March CPS.

NOTE: Statistics reported in this table are sensitive to the consumer
price index, except for the 80/20 ratio.

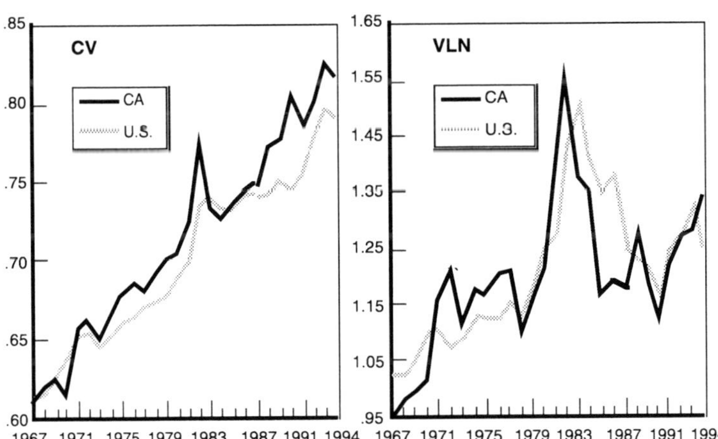

SOURCE: Based on authors' calculations from the March CPS.
NOTE: Statistics reported in this figure are not sensitive to the consumer price index.

Figure C.15—Summary Measures of Inequality for Annual Salary
for Males, 1967–1994

Income Type 22: Annual Earnings Among Female Workers Ages 18 to 55

Table C.18

Percentage Change in Real Annual Earnings for Females Ages 18 to 55 Between Selected Years, by Income Percentile

	Business Cycle Peaks			Recessions
	1969–1979	1979–1989	1969–1989	1976–1994
California				
20th	62	13	83	25
Median	22	6	29	29
80th	11	22	36	30
Change in				
80/20 ratio (%)	–31	+8	–26	+5
United States				
20th	48	24	85	56
Median	19	19	42	25
80th	16	24	44	34
Change in				
80/20 ratio (%)	–22	0	–22	–14

SOURCE: Based on authors' calculations from the March CPS.

NOTE: Statistics reported in this table are sensitive to the consumer price index, except for the 80/20 ratio.

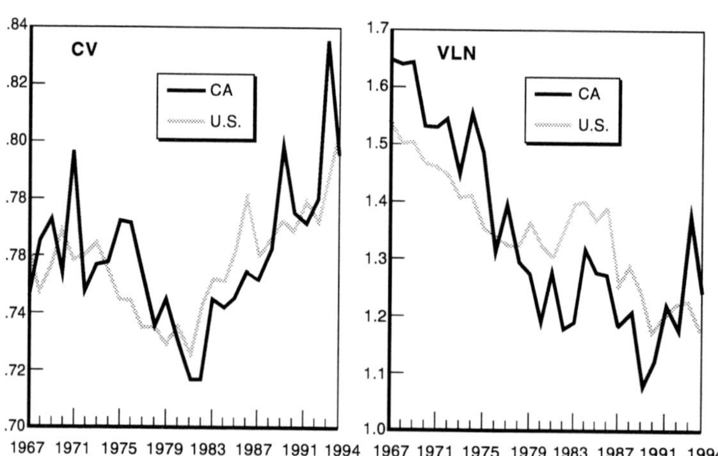

SOURCE: Based on authors' calculations from the March CPS.

NOTE: Statistics reported in this figure are not sensitive to the consumer price index.

Figure C.16—Summary Measures of Inequality for Annual Earnings for Females Ages 18 to 55, 1967–1994

Income Type 23: Hourly Wages Among Female Workers Ages 18 to 55

Table C.19

Percentage Change in Real Hourly Wages for Females Ages 18 to 55 Between Selected Years, by Income Percentile

	Business Cycle Peaks	Recessions
	1979–1989	1976–1994
California		
20th	–9	–7
Median	2	10
80th	15	21
Change in		
80/20 ratio (%)	+27	+31
United States		
20th	–4	–1
Median	8	11
80th	16	22
Change in		
80/20 ratio (%)	+21	+24

SOURCE: Based on authors' calculations from the March CPS.

NOTE: Statistics reported in this table are sensitive to the consumer price index, except for the 80/20 ratio.

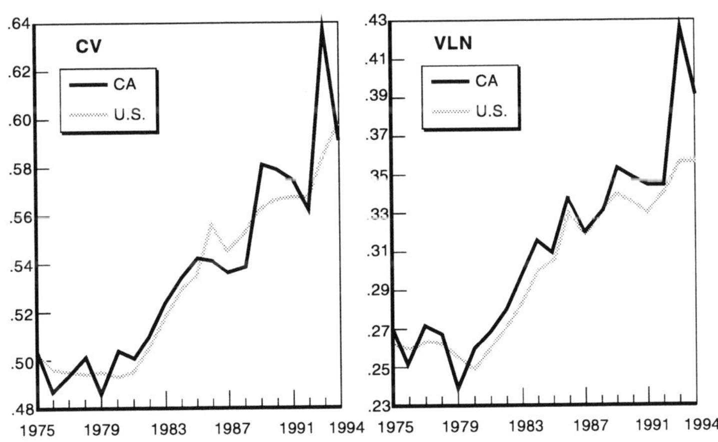

SOURCE: Based on authors' calculations from the March CPS.

NOTE: Statistics reported in this figure are not sensitive to the consumer price index.

Figure C.17—Summary Measures of Inequality for Hourly Wages for Females Ages 18 to 55, 1975–1994

Income Type 24: Annual Earnings Among All Female Workers

Table C.20

Percentage Change in Real Annual Earnings for All Female
Workers Between Selected Years, by Income Percentile

	Business Cycle Peaks			Recessions
	1969–1979	1979–1989	1969–1989	1976–1994
California				
20th	77	12	98	28
Median	22	7	30	27
80th	10	22	35	28
Change in 80/20 ratio (%)	–38	+10	–32	0
United States				
20th	42	30	85	51
Median	21	14	38	24
80th	16	20	39	34
Change in 80/20 ratio (%)	–18	–8	–25	–11

SOURCE: Based on authors' calculations from the March CPS.

NOTE: Statistics reported in this table are sensitive to the consumer price index, except for the 80/20 ratio.

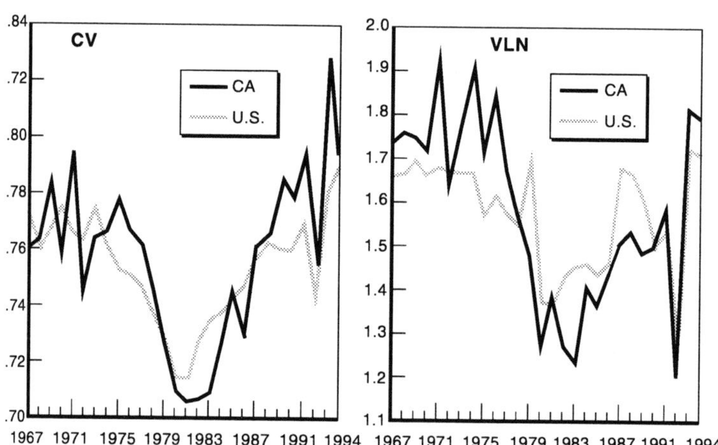

SOURCE: Based on authors' calculations from the March CPS.
NOTE: Statistics reported in this figure are not sensitive to the consumer price index.

Figure C.18—Summary Measures of Inequality for Annual
Earnings for All Female Workers, 1967–1994

Income Type 25: Hourly Wages Among All Female Workers

Table C.21

Percentage Change in Real Hourly Wages for All Female Workers Between Selected Years, by Income Percentile

	Business Cycle Peaks	Recessions
	1979–1989	1976–1994
California		
20th	–9	–8
Median	2	7
80th	15	18
Change in		
80/20 ratio (%)	+26	+28
United States		
20th	–5	–1
Median	10	11
80th	16	22
Change in		
80/20 ratio (%)	+23	+23

SOURCE: Based on authors' calculations from the March CPS.

NOTE: Statistics reported in this table are sensitive to the consumer price index, except for the 80/20 ratio.

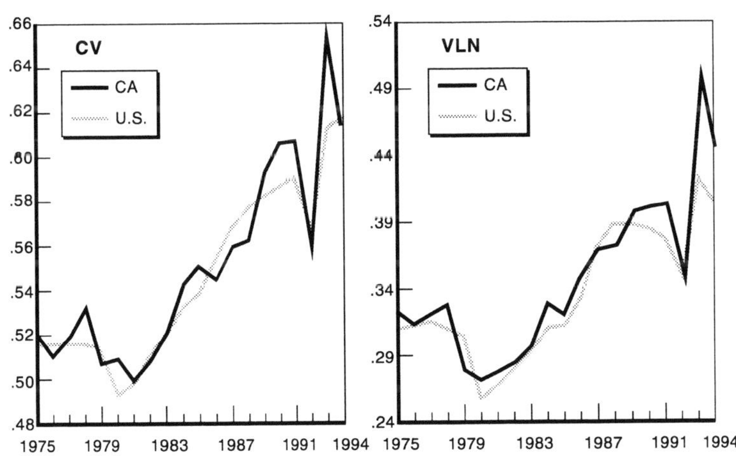

SOURCE: Based on authors' calculations from the March CPS.

NOTE: Statistics reported in this figure are not sensitive to the consumer price index.

Figure C.19—Summary Measures of Inequality for Hourly Wages for All Female Workers, 1975–1994

Table C.22

Percentage Change in Real Annual Salary for Females
Between Selected Years, by Income Percentile

	Business Cycle Peaks			Recessions
	1969–1979	1979–1989	1969–1989	1976–1994
California				
20th	53	23	89	28
Median	22	10	34	27
80th	12	18	33	25
Change in 80/20 ratio (%)	–26	–4	–30	–2
United States				
20th	36	20	64	50
Median	13	15	30	27
80th	12	24	39	30
Change in 80/20 ratio (%)	–18	+4	–15	–14

SOURCE: Based on authors' calculations from the March CPS.

NOTE: Statistics reported in this table are sensitive to the consumer price index, except for the 80/20 ratio.

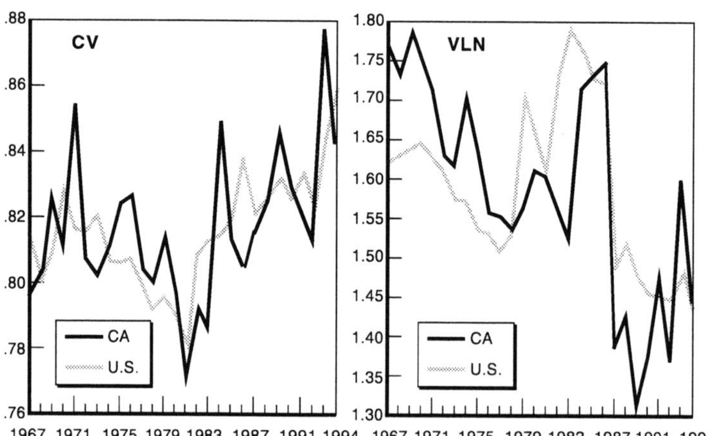

SOURCE: Based on authors' calculations from the March CPS.

NOTE: Statistics reported in this figure are not sensitive to the consumer price index.

Figure C.20—Summary Measures of Inequality for Annual Salary
for Females, 1967–1994

Appendix D

Supplementary Statistics

This appendix provides additional statistics on the trends in the distributions of income for those measures of income discussed in the main text. The appendix contains several tables. Tables D.1 through D.10 show deciles of the distributions of adjusted household income, male annual earnings, male hourly wages, female annual earnings, and female hourly wages. Reported decile levels are in nominal terms. The price index from Table A.1 is provided for cost of living and inflation adjustments (multiply the income level by the price index). Then, Tables D.11 and D.12 show regional comparisons of the coefficient of variation for male and female annual earnings. Finally, Tables D.13 through D.15 give state comparisons of the coefficient of variation for adjusted household income, male annual earnings, and female annual earnings.

Table D.1

Deciles of Nominal Adjusted Household Income, California

Year	10%	20%	30%	40%	50%	60%	70%	80%	90%	Price Index
1967	3499	5281	6720	7989	9236	10651	12408	14901	19249	4.22
1968	3914	5676	7246	8665	10003	11621	13583	16151	21194	4.07
1969	4061	5997	7627	9090	10695	12465	14578	17315	22437	3.91
1969 (C)	3667	5831	7647	9263	10854	12656	14779	17718	22900	3.91
1970	4175	6203	7800	9491	11291	13145	15309	18185	23079	3.76
1971	4159	6179	8030	9785	11485	13266	15448	18976	24496	3.62
1972	4213	6197	8195	10213	12310	14533	17184	20417	26103	3.51
1973	4654	7008	9248	11489	13781	16075	18567	21705	28150	3.31
1974	5074	7419	9855	12262	14633	17017	19610	23145	29210	3.04
1975	5266	8088	10512	13343	15792	18473	21717	26122	33852	2.77
1976	6174	8894	11525	14195	17070	20046	23365	27636	35836	2.61
1977	6692	9442	12278	15500	18712	22007	25788	30645	39637	2.44
1978	7188	10347	13881	17124	20743	24223	28765	34064	44608	2.27
1979	7690	11439	15561	19078	22841	26709	32373	38951	49068	2.08
1979 (C)	7446	11553	15530	19420	23210	27492	32436	39332	50926	2.08
1980	8653	12732	16946	21016	25495	30023	35586	43226	54066	1.84
1981	8516	12874	17139	21451	26840	31797	38266	46669	60000	1.67
1982	8697	13187	17588	22643	27853	33964	41121	50260	64044	1.57
1983	8490	13594	18224	24066	29087	35233	42658	51945	67108	1.53
1984	9903	15561	21220	26308	31441	37827	46015	55472	72588	1.46
1985	10141	15970	22018	27314	33606	40559	48734	59935	78713	1.40
1986	10543	16270	22731	29082	35929	43431	51897	63873	82836	1.35
1987a	11132	17711	24027	30758	36958	44456	53882	67134	88947	1.30
1987	11320	17792	24013	30781	37034	44434	53788	66402	87723	1.30
1988	10825	17669	24144	31056	36850	45152	55029	69489	91351	1.24
1989	12462	18878	25999	33511	40876	49150	58213	72184	96805	1.18
1989 (C)	13101	20500	27944	35330	43070	51962	62367	77000	102615	1.18
1990	12132	19401	26180	34007	41117	49901	61079	75996	100742	1.12
1991	11790	18288	25297	33529	41709	50295	61040	76628	102252	1.08
1992	11787	18771	25718	34583	41924	51974	63210	78740	103648	1.04
1993	11257	17615	24265	31757	39969	50999	64284	81672	107405	1.01
1994	11205	18002	25963	33305	43330	55040	66503	82618	110106	1.00

SOURCE: Authors' calculations from the CPS and Census (C). 1987a is based on the original release of the March 1988 CPS, which used the processing system of previous years.

NOTE: Household income is adjusted for household size: Reported deciles are calibrated to represent a household of four.

Table D.2

Deciles of Nominal Adjusted Household Income, United States

Year	10%	20%	30%	40%	50%	60%	70%	80%	90%	Price Index
1967	2773	4294	5602	6767	7965	9166	10679	12761	16395	4.50
1968	3089	4761	6209	7442	8703	10028	11688	14005	17802	4.33
1969	3380	5220	6784	8169	9579	11077	12888	15337	19639	4.15
1969 (C)	3060	5050	6736	8198	9650	11201	13106	15704	20350	4.15
1970	3511	5465	7072	8546	10019	11664	13625	16260	20791	3.96
1971	3695	5658	7323	8940	10512	12242	14271	17124	21954	3.79
1972	3929	6060	8010	9811	11540	13452	15718	18734	24186	3.68
1973	4319	6713	8851	10740	12595	14710	17232	20530	26047	3.46
1974	4683	7202	9476	11556	13604	15821	18455	22037	28093	3.15
1975	4935	7539	9970	12225	14583	16977	19843	23760	30262	2.91
1976	5373	8246	10783	13362	15916	18566	21721	25729	32682	2.75
1977	5784	8903	11749	14505	17285	20261	23778	28336	35940	2.58
1978	6306	9814	13119	16033	19025	22341	26206	31209	39817	2.42
1979	6938	10807	14475	17882	21220	24935	29240	35033	44182	2.21
1979 (C)	6710	10760	14432	17947	21311	25020	29456	35348	45368	2.21
1980	7320	11559	15422	19255	22909	26892	31756	38110	48264	1.98
1981	7734	12185	16366	20516	24601	29095	34428	41359	52786	1.81
1982	7651	12550	17069	21458	25900	30701	36466	44202	57358	1.71
1983	7953	12837	17657	22321	27043	32260	38378	46739	60170	1.64
1984	8616	14013	19254	24125	29194	34857	41505	50590	65506	1.57
1985	9084	14787	20139	25481	30740	36731	43735	53358	69485	1.52
1986	9375	15503	21222	26813	32372	38620	46086	56253	73222	1.49
1987a	9728	16109	22170	28001	34173	40629	48432	59224	76889	1.44
1987	9865	16269	22382	28300	34471	40860	48852	59469	77557	1.44
1988	10395	17046	23349	29565	35843	42955	51327	62401	82020	1.38
1989	11385	18245	25060	31519	38355	45643	54520	66719	87567	1.32
1989(C)	11314	18779	25470	32000	38682	46052	55007	67199	88912	1.32
1990	11507	18796	25512	32193	39019	46446	55629	68278	89170	1.25
1991	11535	18931	26021	32972	40070	48084	57254	70090	91503	1.20
1992	11641	19142	26256	33499	41121	49384	58902	72078	94658	1.16
1993	11629	19316	26383	33802	41413	50242	60558	75345	99102	1.13
1994	12343	20332	27900	35094	43070	52192	62897	77440	101849	1.10

SOURCE: Authors' calculations from the CPS and Census (C). 1987a is based on the original release of the March 1988 CPS, which used the processing system of previous years.

NOTE: Household income is adjusted for household size: Reported deciles are calibrated to represent a household of four.

Table D.3

Deciles of Nominal Annual Earnings Among Male Workers, California

Year	10%	20%	30%	40%	50%	60%	70%	80%	90%	Price Index
1967	2200	4099	5499	6499	7399	8130	9098	10498	12997	4.22
1968	2434	4496	5994	6994	7993	8992	9991	11689	14303	4.07
1969	2342	4499	6006	7346	8369	9508	10608	12010	15012	3.91
1969 (C)	2150	4550	6050	7350	8450	9650	10750	12050	15050	3.91
1970	2502	4503	6081	7505	8665	9890	11007	12808	15510	3.76
1971	1997	4095	6081	7590	8988	9987	11485	13183	16279	3.62
1972	2231	4498	6447	7997	9496	10995	12095	14294	17893	3.51
1973	2484	4796	6702	8392	9991	11689	12988	14986	18483	3.31
1974	2554	5006	6862	8510	10012	12014	14017	16019	20024	3.04
1975	2797	5106	7358	9411	11012	13015	15017	17520	21424	2.77
1976	2716	5490	7986	9982	11979	14175	16091	18717	22989	2.61
1977	3004	6009	8253	10516	12981	15022	17526	20030	25037	2.44
1978	3506	6793	9490	11987	14385	16622	19127	22234	27471	2.27
1979	3991	7184	9977	12555	15433	17959	20952	24943	30930	2.08
1979 (C)	3805	7005	10005	12505	15435	18205	21005	25005	30505	2.08
1980	4003	7406	10408	13530	16713	20015	23018	26020	34026	1.84
1981	3886	7511	11016	14266	17847	21031	24869	29043	36053	1.67
1982	4008	7514	10520	14327	18034	22042	26049	31059	40076	1.57
1983	4856	8989	12465	15981	19976	23971	27367	32960	41949	1.53
1984	4501	8403	12034	16925	20807	25008	29009	34953	43014	1.46
1985	5018	9032	12545	17061	21813	26093	30107	36128	46164	1.40
1986	5190	9222	12974	17964	22954	27537	31937	37925	48903	1.35
1987a	5411	9953	13739	18020	23512	28515	33991	40021	50026	1.30
1987	5603	9705	13307	18010	23012	28015	33418	40021	50026	1.30
1988	5488	9977	14168	17959	22948	27936	32925	39909	50884	1.24
1989	5822	9970	13957	18418	23927	29410	34894	41872	54833	1.18
1989(C)	6000	10136	15000	19142	24000	29971	35000	41000	52032	1.18
1990	5988	9980	14272	18962	24042	29941	34931	44100	58883	1.12
1991	6014	10023	14032	19316	25057	30069	36083	45103	59136	1.08
1992	5997	9995	14992	19990	24987	30984	38481	45977	60969	1.04
1993	4980	9960	13546	17928	23904	29880	36852	45816	59760	1.01
1994	6000	10400	15000	19200	25000	30772	40000	50000	65000	1.00

SOURCE: Authors' calculations from the CPS and Census (C). 1987a is based on the original release of the March 1988 CPS, which used the processing system of previous years.

118

Table D.4

Deciles of Nominal Annual Earnings Among Male Workers, United States

Year	10%	20%	30%	40%	50%	60%	70%	80%	90%	Price Index
1967	2001	3609	4891	5604	6504	7204	8005	9406	11507	4.50
1968	2101	4001	5002	6002	7002	7803	8960	10003	12004	4.33
1969	2275	4091	5503	6603	7503	8465	9675	11005	13806	4.15
1969 (C)	2150	4050	5450	6550	7550	8550	9850	11050	14050	4.15
1970	2210	4160	5601	6803	7806	8982	10001	11701	14502	3.96
1971	2100	4131	5694	7001	8002	9203	10402	12002	15003	3.79
1972	2403	4596	6072	7510	8911	10013	11415	13017	16521	3.68
1973	2597	5003	6664	8005	9561	11007	12108	14409	18012	3.46
1974	2623	5025	7009	8511	10013	11515	13017	15020	19025	3.15
1975	2745	5133	7218	8985	10482	11980	13976	15973	19966	2.91
1976	2895	5590	7794	9750	11478	13027	14974	17649	21961	2.75
1977	3206	6011	8279	10287	12022	14426	16430	19091	24044	2.58
1978	3661	6691	8988	11083	13476	15579	17976	20772	25267	2.42
1979	3997	7352	9994	11992	14862	16989	19987	22985	28082	2.21
1979 (C)	3905	7125	10005	12005	15005	17025	20005	23005	29005	2.21
1980	4003	7506	10186	13011	15513	18215	21017	25020	30024	1.98
1981	3999	7838	10998	13997	16854	19996	22995	26994	33983	1.81
1982	3911	7521	10730	14039	17047	20055	24066	28077	36100	1.71
1983	4006	7956	11115	14921	18025	21029	25034	30041	38052	1.64
1984	4211	8341	12031	15506	19048	23059	27069	32081	40102	1.57
1985	4809	9017	12524	16031	20039	24047	28054	34066	42082	1.52
1986	4992	9225	12979	16972	20149	24960	29951	34943	44927	1.49
1987a	4982	9868	13741	17618	21245	25411	29895	35874	46317	1.44
1987	4982	9888	13552	17538	20926	25012	29895	35874	45839	1.44
1988	5388	9978	14392	17961	21952	26641	31132	37917	48893	1.38
1989	6024	10543	15061	19077	23093	28113	33134	40162	50202	1.32
1989 (C)	6000	10906	15000	19000	22802	27000	31500	38000	48098	1.32
1990	5979	10603	14948	18935	23419	27904	33385	39863	51323	1.25
1991	5810	10017	15026	19334	24042	29050	35061	41071	53092	1.20
1992	5780	10436	15052	20070	25087	30105	35122	43150	55318	1.16
1993	6026	11047	15064	20086	25107	30129	35652	44189	58249	1.13
1994	6580	12000	16000	20800	25000	30772	37964	46000	60000	1.10

SOURCE: Authors' calculations from the CPS and Census (C). 1987a is based on the original release of the March 1988 CPS, which used the processing system of previous years.

Table D.5

Deciles of Nominal Hourly Wages Among Male Workers, California

Year	10%	20%	30%	40%	50%	60%	70%	80%	90%	Price Index
1975	2.41	3.24	4.09	4.88	5.73	6.35	7.22	8.42	10.38	2.77
1976	2.56	3.52	4.32	5.23	6.08	6.91	7.86	9.05	11.04	2.61
1977	2.70	3.76	4.67	5.54	6.46	7.31	8.35	9.63	11.80	2.44
1978	2.88	3.92	4.99	5.95	6.99	7.99	9.12	10.57	13.09	2.27
1979	3.17	4.32	5.37	6.57	7.67	8.76	10.00	11.51	14.39	2.08
1980	3.46	4.81	5.77	7.11	8.39	9.62	11.07	12.83	15.93	1.84
1981	3.49	4.81	6.08	7.50	8.81	10.30	11.94	13.70	17.33	1.67
1982	3.76	5.01	6.42	7.86	9.63	11.13	12.81	15.07	19.27	1.57
1983	3.84	5.27	6.81	8.34	9.70	11.52	13.28	15.61	19.63	1.53
1984	3.85	5.37	6.93	8.66	10.13	12.02	13.77	16.22	20.20	1.46
1985	3.94	5.44	7.06	9.12	10.72	12.54	14.62	17.37	21.44	1.40
1986	4.08	5.76	7.20	9.12	11.20	13.21	15.35	17.75	22.36	1.35
1987a	4.15	5.77	7.42	9.38	11.42	13.68	15.87	18.76	24.05	1.30
1987	4.17	5.77	7.50	9.38	11.17	13.47	15.49	18.28	23.09	1.30
1988	4.32	5.82	7.48	9.40	11.17	13.43	15.71	19.19	24.55	1.24
1989	4.44	5.98	7.67	9.59	11.56	14.24	16.49	19.82	24.92	1.18
1990	4.57	6.11	7.70	9.60	12.00	14.39	16.79	19.96	26.32	1.12
1991	4.73	6.26	8.19	10.12	12.30	14.55	17.35	21.03	27.34	1.08
1992	4.81	6.53	8.24	10.25	12.88	15.38	18.26	21.97	28.83	1.04
1993	4.64	6.17	7.76	9.85	11.97	14.59	17.62	21.55	28.73	1.01
1994	4.81	6.41	8.33	10.10	12.39	15.38	18.75	23.08	29.62	1.00

SOURCE: Authors' calculations from the March CPS. 1987a is based on the original release of the March 1988 CPS, which used the processing system of previous years.

NOTES: Hourly wages not calculated before 1975 because earlier CPSs did not ask respondents about their hours of work in a usual week in the previous year (annual earnings refers to earnings in the previous year). Hourly wages not calculated for the Census because the 1970 Census also did not ask about weekly hours of work in the previous year.

Table D.6

Deciles of Nominal Hourly Wages Among Male Workers, United States

Year	10%	20%	30%	40%	50%	60%	70%	80%	90%	Price Index
1975	2.36	3.17	3.85	4.57	5.27	5.93	6.72	7.68	9.60	2.91
1976	2.46	3.35	4.08	4.80	5.60	6.37	7.20	8.35	10.24	2.75
1977	2.61	3.56	4.38	5.17	5.99	6.86	7.78	9.02	11.13	2.58
1978	2.84	3.78	4.69	5.52	6.40	7.36	8.45	9.60	12.00	2.42
1979	3.07	4.16	5.09	6.03	7.08	8.17	9.37	10.68	13.15	2.21
1980	3.30	4.47	5.50	6.54	7.70	8.85	10.10	11.84	14.43	1.98
1981	3.47	4.81	5.77	7.02	8.19	9.61	11.06	12.83	15.86	1.81
1982	3.55	4.82	6.05	7.26	8.68	10.03	11.75	13.76	17.08	1.71
1983	3.57	4.90	6.26	7.51	8.83	10.35	12.04	14.35	17.81	1.64
1984	3.67	5.06	6.42	7.71	9.40	11.03	12.66	14.94	18.80	1.57
1985	3.85	5.30	6.74	8.19	9.63	11.48	13.21	15.56	19.27	1.52
1986	3.99	5.46	6.91	8.40	9.98	11.76	13.82	16.22	20.45	1.49
1987a	3.85	5.44	6.87	8.32	9.76	11.56	13.82	16.18	20.21	1.44
1987	4.00	5.70	7.13	8.62	10.12	11.98	14.37	16.77	20.91	1.44
1988	4.23	5.79	7.42	8.97	10.55	12.47	14.47	17.27	21.93	1.38
1989	4.46	6.11	7.72	9.41	11.10	13.03	15.45	18.34	23.17	1.32
1990	4.57	6.23	7.73	9.58	11.24	13.18	15.33	18.69	23.96	1.25
1991	4.67	6.26	8.01	9.63	11.56	13.58	16.11	19.26	24.56	1.20
1992	4.82	6.51	8.20	9.91	12.01	14.23	16.84	19.68	25.57	1.16
1993	4.83	6.53	8.21	9.95	12.05	14.28	16.90	20.21	26.34	1.13
1994	5.00	6.77	8.55	10.22	12.16	14.42	17.31	20.98	27.47	1.10

SOURCE: Authors' calculations from the March CPS. 1987a is based on the original release of the March 1988 CPS, which used the processing system of previous years.

NOTES: Hourly wages not calculated before 1975 because earlier CPSs did not ask respondents about their hours of work in a usual week in the previous year (annual earnings refers to earnings in the previous year). Hourly wages not calculated for the Census because the 1970 Census also did not ask about weekly hours of work in the previous year.

Table D.7

Deciles of Nominal Annual Earnings Among Female Workers, California

Year	10%	20%	30%	40%	50%	60%	70%	80%	90%	Price Index
1967	366	900	1700	2400	3068	3999	4799	5799	6999	4.22
1968	400	999	1698	2498	3397	4196	5015	6011	7493	4.07
1969	375	993	1699	2502	3503	4333	5304	6265	7771	3.91
1969 (C)	450	1050	1950	2950	3750	4650	5550	6550	8050	3.91
1970	450	1006	1871	3002	3903	4815	5904	7005	8223	3.76
1971	399	1011	1804	2796	3941	4994	5992	7040	8988	3.62
1972	520	1299	2234	3287	4498	5498	6697	7797	9796	3.51
1973	599	1399	2318	3312	4396	5695	6994	8117	10091	3.31
1974	601	1464	2467	3504	4601	5857	7008	8589	11013	3.04
1975	701	1511	2729	3954	5050	6507	8009	9570	12013	2.77
1976	799	1996	2995	4193	5450	6988	8485	9982	12877	2.61
1977	929	2003	3294	4807	6009	7511	9013	11016	14021	2.44
1978	999	2399	3896	5095	6793	7992	9989	11987	14984	2.27
1979	1297	2993	4590	5986	7981	9379	10975	12970	17161	2.08
1979 (C)	1305	3005	4505	6005	7875	9505	11005	13465	17365	2.08
1980	1601	3493	5004	7005	9007	10508	12510	15011	19815	1.84
1981	1602	3505	5308	7395	9546	11577	13812	16149	21031	1.67
1982	2004	3866	6011	8015	10019	12263	15029	18034	23044	1.57
1983	1998	4195	6193	8984	10987	12984	15781	19177	24970	1.53
1984	2001	4258	6442	9137	11604	14004	16983	20006	26008	1.46
1985	2007	4215	7025	9706	12143	15053	18064	22078	28602	1.40
1986	1996	4890	7171	9980	12974	15968	18962	22954	29941	1.35
1987a	2401	5003	7804	10506	14005	17009	20011	24513	31016	1.30
1987	2501	5003	7671	10405	13209	16753	20011	24776	31016	1.30
1988	2993	5522	8082	11195	14467	17959	21566	25941	33923	1.24
1989	3274	5982	8773	11964	14954	17945	22930	27915	35891	1.18
1989 (C)	3000	6000	9393	12000	15800	19500	23421	28050	36000	1.18
1990	2994	5988	8982	11976	14970	19960	23952	28943	36927	1.12
1991	3157	6014	9622	12829	16574	20046	25057	30069	38438	1.08
1992	2998	6497	9995	12993	16991	20989	25487	30984	39980	1.04
1993	2789	5976	9362	12948	16932	20916	24900	31872	42828	1.01
1994	3000	6000	10000	13000	18000	23000	28000	34000	43000	1.00

SOURCE: Authors' calculations from the CPS and Census (C). 1987a is based on the original release of the March 1988 CPS, which used the processing system of previous years.

Table D.8

Deciles of Nominal Annual Earnings Among Female Workers, United States

Year	10%	20%	30%	40%	50%	60%	70%	80%	90%	Price Index
1967	300	750	1301	2001	2748	3302	4003	4953	6004	4.50
1968	350	850	1500	2156	3001	3581	4201	5002	6452	4.33
1969	390	925	1578	2371	3107	3912	4647	5527	7003	4.15
1969 (C)	450	1050	1750	2550	3250	4050	4850	5750	7150	4.15
1970	400	1000	1700	2500	3345	4100	5001	6001	7601	3.96
1971	450	1040	1800	2712	3554	4371	5201	6284	8002	3.79
1972	501	1172	2003	3004	3845	4706	5607	6904	8511	3.68
1973	500	1201	2001	3002	4003	5003	6004	7205	9006	3.46
1974	575	1352	2303	3259	4296	5207	6408	7910	9895	3.15
1975	653	1547	2496	3604	4776	5890	6988	8486	10694	2.91
1976	735	1757	2822	3993	5021	6189	7587	9014	11480	2.75
1977	801	2004	3005	4276	5510	6913	8015	10018	12190	2.58
1978	939	2001	3396	4894	5992	7490	8988	10631	13482	2.42
1979	1039	2498	3997	5496	6995	8195	9994	11992	14990	2.21
1979 (C)	1195	2565	4005	5505	7005	8165	10005	12005	15005	2.21
1980	1154	2856	4323	6005	7599	9101	11009	13011	16613	1.98
1981	1300	2999	4879	6499	8098	9998	11997	14497	17996	1.81
1982	1474	3169	5014	7019	9025	10930	13036	15765	20055	1.71
1983	1502	3455	5464	7510	9613	11716	14019	17023	21433	1.64
1984	1540	3609	5922	8020	10025	12031	15038	18046	23059	1.57
1985	1703	3908	6012	8260	10520	13025	15630	19338	25049	1.52
1986	1797	3994	6330	8892	10982	13897	16673	19968	25958	1.49
1987a	1993	4504	6975	9487	11958	14768	17680	20926	27520	1.44
1987	1993	4599	6975	9565	11958	14748	17738	21126	27404	1.44
1988	2130	4989	7284	9978	12473	14967	18459	22950	29517	1.38
1989	2465	5020	8032	10442	13053	16065	20081	24097	31126	1.32
1989 (C)	2500	5219	8000	10500	13110	16000	19917	24000	30130	1.32
1990	2491	5406	8013	10962	13952	16942	20330	24914	31890	1.25
1991	2719	5810	8834	11565	14585	18031	21638	26045	34560	1.20
1992	2950	6021	9031	12042	15052	19066	23080	28098	35508	1.16
1993	3013	6026	9039	12051	15566	19164	23099	29024	37661	1.13
1994	3000	6288	9625	12500	16000	20000	24000	30000	39200	1.10

SOURCE: Authors' calculations from the CPS and Census (C). 1987a is based on the original release of the March 1988 CPS, which used the processing system of previous years.

Table D.9

Deciles of Nominal Hourly Wages Among Female Workers, California

Year	10%	20%	30%	40%	50%	60%	70%	80%	90%	Price Index
1975	1.64	2.19	2.59	3.03	3.49	3.99	4.55	5.29	6.67	2.77
1976	1.86	2.40	2.75	3.24	3.74	4.22	4.80	5.61	6.93	2.61
1977	1.96	2.50	3.00	3.51	3.97	4.51	5.14	6.05	7.54	2.44
1978	2.12	2.79	3.29	3.75	4.32	4.80	5.40	6.38	7.97	2.27
1979	2.49	3.12	3.63	4.21	4.80	5.40	6.21	7.13	9.11	2.08
1980	2.69	3.37	4.07	4.74	5.29	6.00	6.90	8.18	10.13	1.84
1981	2.89	3.61	4.38	5.06	5.78	6.48	7.45	8.82	11.07	1.67
1982	3.01	3.85	4.67	5.32	6.25	7.16	8.19	9.63	12.04	1.57
1983	3.08	4.00	4.82	5.71	6.45	7.37	8.61	10.08	12.64	1.53
1984	3.13	4.15	5.00	5.96	6.84	7.85	9.14	11.04	13.55	1.46
1985	3.35	4.34	5.31	6.27	7.24	8.44	9.76	11.67	14.47	1.40
1986	3.20	4.24	5.33	6.40	7.49	8.73	10.00	12.00	15.21	1.35
1987a	3.46	4.69	5.77	6.83	8.00	9.31	10.63	12.83	16.35	1.30
1987	3.50	4.69	5.77	6.73	7.87	9.24	10.63	12.71	16.03	1.30
1988	3.74	4.88	5.99	7.14	8.39	9.59	11.51	13.43	16.79	1.24
1989	3.83	4.98	6.23	7.48	8.63	10.20	11.98	14.38	18.33	1.18
1990	3.91	5.23	6.39	7.68	9.21	10.59	12.48	14.97	19.19	1.12
1991	4.25	5.57	6.79	8.25	9.64	11.38	13.23	15.69	20.05	1.08
1992	4.32	5.77	7.08	8.65	10.09	11.66	13.45	16.34	20.82	1.04
1993	4.15	5.58	7.11	8.62	10.02	11.92	14.11	17.24	22.03	1.01
1994	4.25	5.77	7.21	8.88	10.58	12.31	14.42	17.31	22.70	1.00

SOURCE: Authors' calculations from the March CPS. 1987a is based on the original release of the March 1988 CPS, which used the processing system of previous years.

NOTES: Hourly wages not calculated before 1975 because earlier CPSs did not ask respondents about their hours of work in a usual week in the previous year (annual earnings refers to earnings in the previous year). Hourly wages not calculated for the Census because the 1970 Census also did not ask about weekly hours of work in the previous year.

Table D.10

Deciles of Nominal Hourly Wages Among Female Workers, United States

Year	10%	20%	30%	40%	50%	60%	70%	80%	90%	Price Index
1975	1.54	2.00	2.38	2.70	3.08	3.50	4.04	4.80	5.87	2.91
1976	1.68	2.20	2.50	2.89	3.33	3.83	4.32	5.05	6.30	2.75
1977	1.78	2.34	2.71	3.13	3.58	4.04	4.68	5.48	6.84	2.58
1978	1.92	2.50	2.92	3.36	3.84	4.32	4.95	5.76	7.24	2.42
1979	2.22	2.88	3.30	3.75	4.26	4.80	5.50	6.44	8.17	2.21
1980	2.41	3.10	3.59	4.09	4.70	5.29	6.01	7.15	8.95	1.98
1981	2.56	3.35	3.85	4.44	5.01	5.77	6.67	7.74	9.77	1.81
1982	2.75	3.50	4.11	4.82	5.41	6.27	7.23	8.56	10.63	1.71
1983	2.86	3.61	4.33	5.01	5.78	6.59	7.70	9.06	11.53	1.64
1984	2.89	3.76	4.47	5.19	6.01	6.91	8.09	9.64	12.05	1.57
1985	3.01	3.85	4.70	5.45	6.26	7.23	8.56	10.12	12.77	1.52
1986	3.00	3.90	4.80	5.67	6.54	7.68	8.89	10.56	13.44	1.49
1987a	3.06	4.01	4.81	5.71	6.68	7.72	9.13	10.72	13.78	1.44
1987	3.19	4.15	4.98	5.92	6.95	8.00	9.49	11.21	14.37	1.44
1988	3.30	4.32	5.28	6.24	7.20	8.50	9.98	11.99	14.97	1.38
1989	3.40	4.59	5.58	6.61	7.72	8.93	10.55	12.55	16.16	1.32
1990	3.65	4.79	5.75	6.79	7.97	9.34	10.95	13.08	16.77	1.25
1991	3.85	5.01	6.01	7.16	8.35	9.63	11.56	13.76	17.53	1.20
1992	3.99	5.14	6.27	7.37	8.68	10.13	12.06	14.47	18.53	1.16
1993	4.02	5.24	6.40	7.73	9.01	10.51	12.31	15.02	19.31	1.13
1994	4.17	5.40	6.50	7.69	9.13	10.72	12.60	15.38	20.13	1.10

SOURCE: Authors' calculations from the March CPS. 1987a is based on the original release of the March 1988 CPS, which used the processing system of previous years.

NOTES: Hourly wages not calculated before 1975 because earlier CPSs did not ask respondents about their hours of work in a usual week in the previous year (annual earnings refers to earnings in the previous year). Hourly wages not calculated for the Census because the 1970 Census also did not ask about weekly hours of work in the previous year.

Table D.11

Regional Trends in the Coefficient of Variation for Real Annual Earnings Among Males, 1969–1994

Region	CV (Rank)				Percentage Change in CV (Rank)		
	1969	1979	1989	1994	1969–1979	1979–1989	1989–1994
California	0.56	0.65	0.75	0.78	15	14	4
	(4)	(2)	(2)	(1)	(3)	(6)	(8)
New England	0.51	0.63	0.65	0.69	25	2	7
	(9)	(4)	(10)	(10)	(1)	(10)	(7)
Mid Atlantic	0.53	0.58	0.67	0.72	9	16	8
	(7)	(9)	(8)	(7)	(6)	(3)	(4)
E. N. Central	0.50	0.54	0.65	0.70	8	19	8
	(10)	(10)	(9)	(8)	(8)	(1)	(3)
W. N. Central	0.52	0.60	0.70	0.69	16	15	0
	(8)	(8)	(5)	(9)	(2)	(4)	(10)
S. Atlantic	0.62	0.66	0.70	0.76	6	6	9
	(1)	(1)	(4)	(4)	(9)	(9)	(1)
E. S. Central	0.62	0.62	0.69	0.74	0	11	7
	(2)	(6)	(6)	(5)	(10)	(8)	(5)
W. S. Central	0.60	0.65	0.77	0.77	9	19	0
	(3)	(3)	(1)	(2)	(7)	(2)	(9)
Mountain	0.54	0.61	0.68	0.73	13	11	8
	(6)	(7)	(7)	(6)	(4)	(7)	(2)
Pacific	0.56	0.62	0.71	0.76	11	15	7
	(5)	(5)	(3)	(3)	(5)	(5)	(6)

SOURCE: Based on authors' calculations from the March CPS.

NOTES: See the notes to Figure 3.1 for sample criteria and the calculation of annual earnings. Statistics reported in this table are not sensitive to the consumer price index.

126

Table D.12

Regional Trends in the Coefficient of Variation for Real Annual Earnings Among Females, 1969–1994

Region	CV (Rank)				Percentage Change in CV (Rank)		
	1969	1979	1989	1994	1969–1979	1979–1989	1989–1994
California	0.78	0.76	0.80	0.81	–3	4	1
	(3)	(3)	(2)	(7)	(4)	(6)	(7)
New England	0.71	0.73	0.76	0.76	2	4	0
	(10)	(5)	(7)	(10)	(2)	(7)	(10)
Mid Atlantic	0.72	0.72	0.78	0.80	0	8	3
	(9)	(8)	(6)	(8)	(3)	(2)	(5)
E. N. Central	0.76	0.72	0.78	0.84	–5	8	8
	(5)	(7)	(5)	(1)	(7)	(3)	(3)
W. N. Central	0.76	0.71	0.80	0.80	–7	12	0
	(6)	(10)	(3)	(9)	(10)	(1)	(9)
S. Atlantic	0.77	0.72	0.76	0.81	–6	6	7
	(4)	(9)	(8)	(5)	(8)	(5)	(4)
E. S. Central	0.75	0.73	0.73	0.81	–3	1	11
	(8)	(6)	(10)	(3)	(5)	(9)	(2)
W. S. Central	0.81	0.75	0.81	0.81	–6	7	1
	(1)	(4)	(1)	(4)	(9)	(4)	(8)
Mountain	0.76	0.79	0.74	0.84	4	–6	12
	(7)	(1)	(9)	(2)	(1)	(10)	(1)
Pacific	0.80	0.76	0.79	0.81	–4	4	2
	(2)	(2)	(4)	(6)	(6)	(8)	(6)

SOURCE: Based on authors' calculations from the March CPS.

NOTES: See the notes to Figure 3.1 for sample criteria and the calculation of annual earnings. Statistics reported in this figure are not sensitive to the consumer price index.

State Rankings for Adjusted Household Income Inequality Based on the Coefficient of Variation: Census

State	1969 CV	1969 Rank	1989 CV	1989 Rank	Change Percent	Change Rank
Alabama	0.71	4	0.71	6	0	43
Alaska	0.65	15	0.62	37	−4	49
Arizona	0.65	15	0.70	8	8	12
Arkansas	0.70	5	0.70	8	1	42
California	0.63	21	0.71	6	13	2
Colorado	0.62	23	0.66	20	6	21
Connecticut	0.57	42	0.62	37	7	15
Delaware	0.60	28	0.61	43	3	32
Florida	0.69	6	0.69	13	0	43
Georgia	0.69	6	0.70	8	2	38
Hawaii	0.59	34	0.61	43	4	28
Idaho	0.60	28	0.64	27	7	15
Illinois	0.60	28	0.67	16	13	2
Indiana	0.56	47	0.61	43	9	9
Iowa	0.60	28	0.62	37	3	32
Kansas	0.62	23	0.65	22	5	25
Kentucky	0.68	9	0.70	8	3	32
Louisiana	0.73	2	0.76	1	5	25
Maine	0.57	42	0.60	46	6	21
Maryland	0.61	26	0.63	32	3	32
Massachusetts	0.57	42	0.63	32	10	7
Michigan	0.57	42	0.65	22	15	1
Minnesota	0.59	34	0.62	37	6	21
Mississippi	0.78	1	0.76	1	−3	48
Missouri	0.65	15	0.67	16	3	32
Montana	0.61	26	0.65	22	7	15
Nebraska	0.63	21	0.62	37	−1	46
Nevada	0.59	34	0.64	27	8	12
New Hampshire	0.55	50	0.57	50	4	28
New Jersey	0.58	38	0.63	32	7	15
New Mexico	0.72	3	0.74	4	2	38
New York	0.65	15	0.73	5	12	4
North Carolina	0.64	20	0.66	20	2	38
North Dakota	0.62	23	0.64	27	2	38
Ohio	0.57	42	0.64	27	11	6
Oklahoma	0.65	15	0.70	8	7	15

Table D.13—continued

State	1969		1989		Change	
	CV	Rank	CV	Rank	Percent	Rank
Oregon	0.60	28	0.65	22	9	19
Pennsylvania	0.58	38	0.65	22	12	4
Rhode Island	0.60	28	0.62	37	3	32
South Carolina	0.69	6	0.67	16	–2	46
South Dakota	0.68	9	0.64	27	–6	50
Tennessee	0.67	12	0.69	13	4	28
Texas	0.68	9	0.75	3	10	7
Utah	0.56	47	0.60	46	8	12
Vermont	0.58	38	0.60	46	4	28
Virginia	0.67	12	0.67	16	0	43
Washington	0.58	38	0.63	32	9	9
West Virginia	0.66	14	0.69	13	5	25
Wisconsin	0.56	47	0.60	46	7	15
Wyoming	0.59	34	0.63	32	6	21

SOURCE: Authors' calculations from the 1970 and 1990 Census.

NOTES: Ties in rank are reported with the highest common rank. For example, if two states are tied for first, both states are reported with rank 1 and the next highest state is reported with rank 3. The CV values for California reported in this table are lower than reported in the text due to top-coding differences. A greater amount of top-coding was required to achieve consistency across all states than was required for consistency between California and the nation as a whole. For consistent comparison across states, adjusted household income was top-coded at 4 percent in each state. The top-code used in the text figures was 2.42 percent. The CV values reported in the text are more accurate for California; the values above are more accurate for comparison with other states.

Table D.14

State Rankings for Male Annual Earnings Inequality Based on the Coefficient of Variation: Census

State	1969 CV	1969 Rank	1989 CV	1989 Rank	Change Percent	Change Rank
Alabama	0.60	7	0.63	15	5	40
Alaska	0.57	15	0.63	15	10	31
Arizona	0.56	18	0.67	3	20	6
Arkansas	0.61	6	0.64	8	4	43
California	0.55	21	0.67	3	22	1
Colorado	0.54	26	0.64	8	18	12
Connecticut	0.53	30	0.59	35	11	30
Delaware	0.55	21	0.58	42	5	40
Florida	0.63	2	0.66	5	4	43
Georgia	0.62	3	0.63	15	2	48
Hawaii	0.53	30	0.60	30	13	22
Idaho	0.53	30	0.61	25	16	14
Illinois	0.51	40	0.61	25	19	9
Indiana	0.48	49	0.58	42	22	1
Iowa	0.52	35	0.58	42	12	24
Kansas	0.55	21	0.60	30	9	33
Kentucky	0.57	15	0.64	8	12	24
Louisiana	0.60	7	0.66	5	10	31
Maine	0.52	35	0.56	47	8	36
Maryland	0.56	18	0.59	35	5	40
Massachusetts	0.52	35	0.58	42	12	24
Michigan	0.50	43	0.60	30	21	4
Minnesota	0.52	35	0.59	35	15	16
Mississippi	0.67	1	0.66	5	−3	50
Missouri	0.56	18	0.63	15	12	24
Montana	0.53	30	0.64	8	20	6
Nebraska	0.55	21	0.60	30	8	36
Nevada	0.54	26	0.62	22	16	14
New Hampshire	0.49	46	0.56	47	14	14
New Jersey	0.54	26	0.61	25	13	22
New Mexico	0.62	3	0.69	1	12	24
New York	0.55	21	0.63	15	15	16
North Carolina	0.59	10	0.61	25	3	47
North Dakota	0.58	13	0.64	8	9	33
Ohio	0.48	49	0.59	35	22	1
Oklahoma	0.57	15	0.64	8	14	14

130

Table D.14—continued

State	1969		1989		Change	
	CV	Rank	CV	Rank	Percent	Rank
Oregon	0.51	40	0.62	22	20	6
Pennsylvania	0.50	43	0.59	35	19	9
Rhode Island	0.52	35	0.57	46	9	33
South Carolina	0.58	13	0.61	25	4	43
South Dakota	0.59	10	0.62	22	4	43
Tennessee	0.59	10	0.63	15	8	36
Texas	0.60	7	0.68	2	14	19
Utah	0.50	43	0.60	30	19	9
Vermont	0.51	40	0.56	47	8	36
Virginia	0.62	3	0.63	15	2	48
Washington	0.49	46	0.59	35	21	4
West Virginia	0.54	26	0.64	8	18	12
Wisconsin	0.49	46	0.56	47	15	16
Wyoming	0.53	30	0.59	35	12	24

SOURCE: Authors' calculations from the 1970 and 1990 Census.

NOTES: Ties in rank are reported with the highest common rank. For example, if two states are tied for first, both states are reported with rank 1 and the next highest state is reported with rank 3. The CV values for California reported in this table are lower than reported in the text due to top-coding differences. A greater amount of top-coding was required to achieve consistency across all states than was required for consistency between California and the nation as a whole. For consistent comparison across states, adjusted household income was top-coded at 4 percent in each state. The top-code used in the text figures was 0.93 percent. The CV values reported in the text are more accurate for California; the values above are more accurate for comparison with other states.

State Rankings for Female Annual Earnings Inequality Based on the Coefficient of Variation: Census

State	1969		1989		Change	
	CV	Rank	CV	Rank	Percent	Rank
Alabama	0.73	18	0.70	13	–5	23
Alaska	0.79	5	0.69	17	–13	48
Arizona	0.74	15	0.70	13	–7	37
Arkansas	0.69	32	0.68	24	–2	12
California	0.70	29	0.69	17	–1	9
Colorado	0.73	18	0.69	17	–6	29
Connecticut	0.65	46	0.63	45	–2	12
Delaware	0.69	32	0.65	39	–6	29
Florida	0.72	22	0.67	31	–7	37
Georgia	0.70	29	0.68	24	–3	15
Hawaii	0.67	39	0.62	49	–6	29
Idaho	0.79	5	0.74	2	–6	29
Illinois	0.65	46	0.67	31	4	1
Indiana	0.68	36	0.69	17	1	6
Iowa	0.75	10	0.67	31	–10	46
Kansas	0.73	18	0.68	24	–7	37
Kentucky	0.69	32	0.71	9	3	3
Louisiana	0.77	7	0.72	5	–6	29
Maine	0.71	25	0.65	39	–8	42
Maryland	0.69	32	0.63	45	–9	44
Massachusetts	0.67	39	0.63	45	–5	23
Michigan	0.71	25	0.73	4	3	3
Minnesota	0.72	22	0.66	37	–8	42
Mississippi	0.76	9	0.70	13	–7	37
Missouri	0.68	36	0.69	17	1	6
Montana	0.77	7	0.72	5	–6	29
Nebraska	0.75	10	0.68	24	–9	44
Nevada	0.66	42	0.66	37	–1	9
New Hampshire	0.66	42	0.62	49	–5	23
New Jersey	0.66	42	0.65	39	–1	9
New Mexico	0.80	2	0.74	2	–6	29
New York	0.65	46	0.68	24	4	1
North Carolina	0.65	46	0.63	45	–3	15
North Dakota	0.81	1	0.70	13	–14	49
Ohio	0.70	29	0.69	17	–2	12
Oklahoma	0.75	10	0.71	9	–4	21

Table D.15—continued

State	1969		1989		Change	
	CV	Rank	CV	Rank	Percent	Rank
Oregon	0.75	10	0.71	9	–5	23
Pennsylvania	0.66	42	0.68	24	2	5
Rhode Island	0.67	39	0.64	43	–5	23
South Carolina	0.65	46	0.65	39	0	8
South Dakota	0.80	2	0.67	31	–17	50
Tennessee	0.68	36	0.67	31	–3	15
Texas	0.73	18	0.71	9	–3	15
Utah	0.74	15	0.72	5	–3	15
Vermont	0.72	22	0.64	43	–11	47
Virginia	0.71	25	0.68	24	–3	15
Washington	0.74	15	0.69	17	–7	37
West Virginia	0.75	10	0.72	5	–4	21
Wisconsin	0.71	25	0.67	31	–5	23
Wyoming	0.80	2	0.75	1	–6	29

SOURCE: Authors' calculations from the 1970 and 1990 Census.

NOTES: Ties in rank are reported with the highest common rank. For example, if two states are tied for first, both states are reported with rank 1 and the next highest state is reported with rank 3. The CV values for California reported in this table are lower than reported in the text due to top-coding differences. A greater amount of top-coding was required to achieve consistency across all states than was required for consistency between California and the nation as a whole. For consistent comparison across states, adjusted household income was top-coded at 4 percent in each state. The top-code used in the text figures was 0.13 percent. The CV values reported in the text are more accurate for California; the values above are more accurate for comparison with other states.

Bibliography

Aaron, Henry (1978), *Politics and the Professors: The Great Society in Perspective*, Brookings Institution, Washington, D.C.

Blinder, Alan (1980), "The Levels and Distribution of Economic Well-Being: Introduction and Preview," in Martin Feldstein (ed.), *The American Economy in Transition*, University of Chicago Press, Chicago.

Borjas, George, Richard Freeman, and Larry Katz (1992), "On the Labor Market Effects of Immigration and Trade," in George Borjas and Richard Freeman (eds.), *Immigration and the Work Force: Economic Consequences for the United States and Source Areas*, University of Chicago Press, Chicago.

Burtless, Gary (1996), "Trends in the Level and Distribution of U.S. Living Standards, 1973–1993," unpublished manuscript, Brookings Institution, Washington, D.C.

Butcher, Kristine, and David Card (1991), "Immigration and Wages: Evidence from the 1980s," *American Economic Review*, Vol. 81, No. 2, May 1991, pp. 292–296.

California Department of Finance (1995), *Statistical Abstract 1995*, Sacramento, California.

Cancian, Maria, Sheldon Danziger, and Peter Gottschalk (1993), "Working Wives and Family Income Inequality Among Married Couples," in Sheldon Danziger and Peter Gottschalk (eds.), *Uneven Tides: The Rising Inequality in America,* Russell Sage Foundation, New York, pp. 195–221.

Cassidy, J. (1995), "Who Killed the Middle Class?" *The New Yorker,* October 16, pp. 113–124.

Center for the Continuing Study of the California Economy (1994), *California Economic Growth—1994 Edition,* Palo Alto, California.

Chamberlain, Jay D., and Phil Spillberg (1991), "Trends in the Distribution of Income and Personal Income Tax Burden for California Taxpayers," *Occasional Papers Series,* California Franchise Tax Board, FTB/OPS 91-01, Sacramento, California.

Cutler, David M., and Larry F. Katz (1991), "Macroeconomic Performance and the Disadvantaged," *Brookings Papers on Economic Activity,* Vol. 2, pp. 1–61.

Cutler, David M., and Larry F. Katz (1992), "Rising Inequality? Changes in the Distribution of Income and Consumption in the 1980s," *American Economic Review,* Vol. 82, No. 2, pp. 546–551.

Danziger, Sheldon, and Peter Gottschalk (1995), *America Unequal,* Russell Sage Foundation, New York.

Freeman, Richard (1993), "How Much Has Deunionization Contributed to the Rise in Male Earnings Inequality?" in Sheldon Danziger and Peter Gottschalk (eds.), *Uneven Tides: The Rising Inequality in America,* Russell Sage Foundation, New York, pp. 133–163.

Gottschalk, Peter, and Robert Moffitt (1994), "The Growth of Earnings Instability in the U.S. Labor Market," *Brookings Papers on Economic Activity,* Vol. 2, pp. 217–272.

Gramlich, Edward M., Robert Kasten, and Frank Sammartino (1993), "Growing Inequality in the 1980s: The Role of Federal Taxes and Cash Transfers," in Sheldon Danziger and Peter Gottschalk (eds.),

Uneven Tides: Rising Inequality in America, Russell Sage Foundation, New York, pp. 225–249.

Hungerford, Thomas (1993), "U.S. Income Mobility in the Seventies and Eighties," *Review of Income and Wealth*, Vol. 39, No. 4, pp. 403–417.

Husted, Thomas (1991), "Changes in State Income Inequality from 1981 to 1987," *The Review of Regional Studies*, Vol. 21, No. 3, pp. 249–260.

Juhn, Chinhui, Kevin M. Murphy, and Brooks Pierce (1993), "Wage Inequality and the Rise in the Return to Skill," *Journal of Political Economy*, Vol. 101, June, pp. 410–442.

Karoly, Lynn (1993), "The Trend in Inequality Among Families, Individuals, and Workers in the United States: A Twenty-Five Year Perspective," in Sheldon Danziger and Peter Gottschalk (eds.), *Uneven Tides: Rising Inequality in America*, Russell Sage Foundation, New York, pp. 19–97.

Karoly, Lynn (1995), unpublished testimony prepared for the California Legislature Assembly Committee on Labor and Employment, October 23.

Karoly, Lynn, and Jacob Alex Klerman (1994), "Using Regional Data to Reexamine the Contribution of Demographic and Sectoral Changes to Increasing U.S. Wage Inequality," in J. H. Bergstrand, T. F. Cosimano, J. W. Houck, and R. G. Sheehan (eds.), *The Changing Distribution of Income in an Open U.S. Economy*, North-Holland, Amsterdam, pp. 183–216.

Karoly, Lynn, and Gary Burtless (1995), "Demographic Change, Rising Earnings Inequality, and the Distribution of Personal Well-Being, 1959–1989," *Demography*, Vol. 32, No. 3, pp. 379–405.

Krueger, Alan (1993), "How Computers Have Changed the Wage Structure: Evidence from Microdata, 1984–89," *Quarterly Journal of Economics*, Vol. 108, February, pp. 33–60.

Levy, Frank (1987), *Dollars and Dreams: The Changing American Income Distribution*, Russell Sage Foundation, New York.

Levy, Frank, and Richard J. Murnane (1992), "U.S. Earnings Levels and Earnings Inequality: A Review of Recent Trends and Proposed Explanations," *Journal of Economic Literature*, Vol. 30, September, pp. 1333–1381.

McMahon, Walter (1991), "Geographical Cost of Living Differences: An Update," *AREUEA Journal*, Vol. 19, No. 3, pp. 426–450.

Pechman, Joseph A. (1990), "The Future of the Income Tax," *American Economic Review*, Vol. 80, No. 1, pp. 1–20.

Topel, Robert (1994), "Regional Labor Markets and the Determinants of Wage Inequality," *American Economic Review*, Vol. 84, No. 2, pp. 17–22.

U.S. Bureau of the Census (1990), *Current Population Reports*, Series P-60, Washington, D.C.

U.S. Bureau of the Census (1994), *Statistical Abstract of the United States*, Washington, D.C.

U.S. Bureau of the Census (1996), *Current Population Reports*, P-60-191, Washington, D.C.

U.S. Bureau of Labor Statistics (1982), "Family Budgets for 1981: Final Report," *Monthly Labor Review*, U.S. Department of Labor, Washington, D.C.

U.S. Department of Commerce and the U.S. Bureau of the Census (1978), *The Current Population Survey: Design and Methodology*, January, Washington, D.C.

U.S. House of Representatives, Committee on Ways and Means (1989), "Trends in Family Income and Income Inequality," *Background Material and Data on Programs Within the Jurisdiction of the Committee on Ways and Means*, U.S. Government Printing Office, Washington, D.C.

Williamson, Jeffrey, and Peter Lindert (1980), *American Inequality: A Macroeconomic History*, Academic Press, New York.

About the Authors

DEBORAH S. REED

Deborah Reed, a research fellow at the Public Policy Institute of California, is a specialist in labor economics and development resources. Her research interests include labor markets, public policy, and poverty in the United States and Brazil. Reed recently completed a post-doctoral fellowship at the Population Studies Center at the University of Michigan. A recipient of fellowships from the Mellon Foundation and Yale University, she has served as a consultant for the World Bank in addition to her teaching and research activities.

Reed received an A.B. (1989) in economics from the University of California, Berkeley, and an M.A. (1990) in economics from Yale University. She will receive her Ph.D. in economics from Yale University in 1996.

MELISSA GLENN HABER

Melissa Glenn Haber is a research assistant at the Public Policy Institute of California. Before joining PPIC, Haber was a research associate at the Family Welfare Research Group where she developed a cost-benefit model to evaluate a state-wide teen pregnancy prevention program funded by the California Office of Family Planning. While at the Research Group, she also produced a report summarizing the cost, causes, and incidence of adolescent childbearing in the United States and in California.

Haber received a B.A. (1991) in comparative religion from Harvard University and a Master's degree in Public Policy (1995) from the University of California, Berkeley.

LAURA A. MAMEESH

Laura Mameesh is a research assistant at the Public Policy Institute of California. She has worked for Los Angeles Mayor Richard Riordan on a business tax relief policy aimed at retaining targeted industries in Los Angeles. Her analysis included calculating the cost to the city of providing tax relief as well as researching the cost of doing business in Los Angeles compared with competitor cities. Prior to her work in Los Angeles, Mameesh worked at the Law & Economics Consulting Group on anti-trust cases.

Mameesh received her B.A. (1990) in economics from Mills College and is near completion of a Master's degree in Public Policy from the University of Southern California.